The Hanging Gardens of East Mulberry Street

and other stories of domestic valor.

Mark Kinsler

These columns appeared in the Lancaster (Ohio) Eagle-Gazette
in 2005, 2006, 2007, and 2008.

Many thanks go to Antoinette Taylor-Thomas, my first editor at the Eagle-Gazette, who gave me a chance to write.

And to Natalie, who inspires everything I do.

ISBN-13: 978-1494781361

ISBN-10: 1494781360

These columns written by Mark Kinsler are reprinted herein by permission of the Lancaster Eagle-Gazette, for whom they were originally written.

It Looks a Whole Lot Easier When You're Standing on the Ground.

Our roof worried me. It did not leak, but there were scary-looking repairs made with tin sheets in the 1930's, and there were pieces of slate in the gutters. They told me at the hardware store that a slate roof will last 100 years, but our place was probably built around 1891. Many of our neighbors had replaced their roofs with shingles, but Natalie liked the old slate.

So one bright summer day, fortified with several hours of library research on the care and repair of slate roofs, I climbed up to have a look.

It sure didn't look that steep from the ground. It was slippery, and I tried to use a sort of modified Australian crawl to go higher. It didn't work. I slid slowly, inexorably down the side, stopping only when my toes hooked into the rickety gutter. The problem then became one of thermal conductivity: the slate tiles had been baking in the sun for hours, and my stomach began to adhere to the century-old surface without benefit of Pam Non-Stick Cooking Spray.

I couldn't get to my feet because the slates are fragile and will break when you walk on them. And if you step on one that breaks you'll find yourself riding a little slate sled, zipping down the roof and over the edge on your way to long-term convalescence.

Thus endeth the First Voyage. The next assault on the summit would require a proper foothold.

I thought about pictures of sailors climbing a cargo net up the side of a ship, and I remembered that I had once purchased, on impulse from Harbor Freight Tools, a 600-foot reel of yellow rope.

The cargo net I made in the back yard didn't look too bad. It was to hang down the slope of the roof, supported by a line of deck screws I put into the roof ridge.

The day of the test dawned clear and bright. I climbed up, carrying the net, looking like Neptune, God of the Sea, had gone into the roofing business. I flung the net over the protruding deck screws, gave it a test tug, and set out.

It was terrible. The net deformed into an interesting shape that closed up the holes and entangled my feet. I nearly became a permanent ornament up there. Our neighbor, a patient fellow who put up with my oddities with great grace until the day he suddenly moved out, stood in his back yard watching The Amazing Kinsler. I'm sure he was just standing by for safety reasons. Otherwise he could have sold tickets.

When Spiderman tried out his new home-made slate-removing tool, he found that the nails were hardened steel and that a slate roof is put together like the monthly mathematics puzzle in Scientific American. I had to go back up with a piece of aluminum sheet to repair the hole I'd made. It looked terrible.

Our roofer said that our roof was made of marvelous Vermont slate and simply needed some maintenance. He arrived with a vigorous crew and a truck full of new roof stuff like flashings and 'drip edge,' and I was stunned at how much needed to be done and how little I knew about doing it. They walked up and down that roof like the noble Iroquois, just how I do not know. They, in turn, do not know who the heck put those screws into the roof ridge, and they were polite enough not to inquire.

The roof looks splendid. Now I've got to figure out what to do with the net.

The Hanging Gardens of East Mulberry Street

We saw another house for sale on our walk last night, and once again Natalie had to reassure me that its family hadn't moved away because of our front yard.

Five years ago I dug up the front lawn to plant a ground cover, either ivy for classiness or Virginia creeper, which grew in Cleveland Heights and turned bright red in the fall.

We started off with ivy. Guangdong Agricultural Brigade #1 labored in the hot sun, planting forty little peat pots of the stuff. We waited, watered and fussed over it every day, but the little ivy sprigs, despondent at their fate, stared blankly into space and would not grow.

Then we had to go away for a couple of weeks. We were glad to get home, but the feeling was not mutual: the front yard was a wasteland, with clumps of grass and some twigs that might once have been ivy. Tara from next door had watched and watered it, but it was not to be: those plants were erased from the Book of Life before they ever got to the checkout.

Our doctor, an avid landscaper, prescribed harlequin plants. Its visual attractiveness was a matter of some debate, but nothing could kill it, said she. So we cleared the playing field with a bottle of Round-Up, giving each withered ivy plant a couple of extra shots to put it out of its misery and planted our harlequins, which followed the ivy into eternal life after about a month.

Driven by pluck, courage, and the prospect of a visit from the code-enforcement officer, I soldiered on. I would try Virginia creeper, but a local variety that could grow anywhere. A massive thicket of the stuff had taken over a field behind Meijer's, so one day on my shortcut M. Kinsler, horticulturist, appropriated about eight pounds of the stuff and planted the cuttings.

Hooray: for the Lord did favor them, and they grew fat, and prospered, re-rooting themselves at intervals. The soil was covered at last, and with the same kind of plant, mostly.

I was less delighted when I considered the East Mulberry Street Experimental Installation objectively from across the street. It looked just terrible, with big jagged leaves and an occasional branch sticking straight up from the undergrowth. But wait; wait until fall, when the leaves turn their glorious red.

And it would have been stunning if I had chosen the Ruby Red cultivar instead of the Turn Brown And Fall Off kind. We sighed and waited for the merciful snows of winter to cover my handiwork.

Zombie Ivy! They couldn't kill it! Watch it return from the dead, decayed peat pots hanging from its ever-lengthening runners!

By summer the resurrected ivy and the grizzled Virginia creeper were battling it out for our fifty square feet of Fairfield County. The creeper tried to shade the ivy with its big leaves, but it had blown off botany class down in Virginia and didn't know that ivy likes shade. With the ivy ascendant and the creeper uglier than ever, I decided that the creeper had to go.

Calling upon years of electronic-repair experience, I traced each tangled creeper stem like a power-supply line down to its deepest roots. Grab and pull: sprigs of creeper jerked down into the ground to my maniacal laughter.

All is quiet now. When nettles occasionally manage to push through the forest canopy, I go into my weeding frenzy, rooting rhinoceros-like for every weed within reach. The grass is gone, the dandelions nearly so, and everything is overrun with luxuriant ivy.

Well, almost everything: the harlequin plants are back.

Kittens vs. Rational Thought: A Behavioral Study

As a calm, competent woman, it is Natalie's job to protect our home from my impulsive folly. Through her wise counsel we live in a modest, attractive house instead of, say, a converted Pullman car, which would have been my choice. She insisted on real carpeting instead of a pallet-load of carpet samples tacked down side by side. On trips we are undoubtedly more comfortable in a motel than on the car mattresses I was going to invent. She keeps our lives centered and sensible in spite of my eccentricities.

For example, whenever I see an ad for free kittens, or see one peering out of box or cage mewing for an adoptive home, I instantly want a kitten. It is then Natalie's duty to point out that we already have two irascible alley cats at home on East Mulberry Street, creatures whose wellspring of tolerance for a new cat would prove negligible. That is why we have two cats, instead of many cats.

But this week the family manual suddenly seems to be missing a section. It was probably five weeks ago that the miracle of life came to a hole under the house next door, and now there are four tiny black kittens and my Natalie is besotted.

She watches from our dining room window. "Ooh," she cries, signifying that the mother cat, a fluffy black creature with cool green eyes and auburn highlights in her luxurious coat, is bringing out the family. Sometimes they hide behind a nearby bush (Natalie detests that bush: I won't let her cut it down) but most days Mrs Cat lounges serenely in the sunlight, proudly watching her kittens tumble over the leaves, locked in mortal combat with one another. She dozes off, patiently tolerating her little ones' somersaults upon her head. They are indeed the most charming of cat families.

"I will hand-feed them," proclaimed Natalie, having done nothing of the sort in her life, "so they will get used to people." Cats love her, but those born outside survive by trusting nobody. I have found her looking longingly down into their burrow.

I didn't realize until today the extent to which matters had deteriorated. "My mother, up in Heaven, would know if I had seven cats," she suddenly observed on our walk this afternoon. "And she would frown at me." I replied that this was very likely correct: my late mother-in-law loved all creatures, but not in the house. I added that a day or two with seven head of fuzzy livestock running through our little home would blunt our enthusiasm as well. And I am in charge of the litter box.

Each day Natalie keeps vigil at the Kitten Observation Post, periodically muttering at me, gesticulating and pointing her little finger in the air in imitation of the pointy tails of the tiny creatures she desires. She is certain that the mother would make a wonderful house cat.

And so the two resident cats and I have a problem. I, too, am sorely tempted by the kittens and their mother, but there would be seven cats. Seven. We can't do it. Our alley abounds with cats, and I wish we could buy a jar of Purina Spay-n-Neuter Chew Treats with New Tuna Flavor and Enhanced Hormone Treatments, but Kroger seems to be out of stock.

I'm sure it will work out, though. The mother cat seems a level-headed creature who will find appropriate placements for her kittens, and there's also a good chance that at some point my beloved wife will recover her wits.

Or, we can move to a farm.

Your Reliable Source for Music and News

I finally bought a good frame for my favorite diploma. It's from a correspondence school: National Radio Institute, of Washington, DC.

I was a 22-year-old Ohio State dropout living in Madison, Wisconsin and I needed a marketable skill. So I sent NRI their $212.00 and began a year of concentrated study, reading lessons and building lab kits. Finally in 1970 I drove to Chicago, where in a great room filled with old Morse code equipment I passed the test for the coveted FCC First Class license. A Madison radio station—WTSO, 1070 On Your Dial—hired me as a transmitter engineer.

WTSO's transmitter building was twelve miles from the studio. It looked like an old hunting lodge, with a couch that reeked of tobacco smoke. No female had ever set foot in the place. The gray-enameled ten-thousand-watt RCA transmitter, its vacuum tubes the size of wastebaskets, stretched across one wall. Copper cables, four inches thick, ran out to six towers planted on our twelve acres of Wisconsin farmland. So great was the power that I could stand outside on a summer night, the red lights blinking two hundred feet above, and hear the antenna coils sing the station's ID jingle.

The job was pretty easy. We turned the transmitter on at 5:00 AM and off at 1:00 AM, and adjusted the power at sunrise and sunset. We kept a log of the advertisements so our sponsors would know that their money was not spent in vain. We kept a log of the transmitter power to assure the FCC that we weren't trying to broadcast Nat "King" Cole to Great Britain. We ran the tapes for Oral Roberts and The Old Time Religion Hour. We set up the delay for the nightly talk show and sat at the switch to cut off the legions of drunks who called in each evening.

And we did the tests of the Emergency Broadcast System, which back in the two-fisted days of the Soviet Union warned of nuclear attack, not thunderstorms. It was during a mid-morning music show that I found the two tapes in a drawer, marked "EBS TEST" and "DO NOT PLAY" respectively. I was bored, and alone, and the angels awaited my next move.

Every tape machine at a radio station has a switch that you can set to make it play either out onto the air (LINE), or only into a little speaker (AUD). I flipped the switch to AUD, inserted "DO NOT PLAY" and pushed the red button. "This is an attack warning," said the voice of one of our announcers. "An actual attack on the United States has been detected."

And then I looked again, and saw that the switch wasn't quite right. Yep: I had just played Attack Warning over the air, mixed with the music of Karen and Richard Carpenter.

An old engineer told me that when you do something really horrible on live radio, the best policy is to just continue on as if nothing happened, because most people won't believe they really heard it anyway. I guess that's true, because nobody ever complained about hearing Doomsday behind "Rainy Days and Mondays."

A few months afterwards, I moved to Connecticut. WTSO is still on the air, rebroadcasting ESPN's audio signal. The new transmitter is controlled by a computer, and nobody works at the transmitter building anymore.

National Radio Institute closed in 1990. But I've kept all of the lessons, including the one in which I learned that sometimes—sometimes—you can get away with something really dumb.

The Thoughtful Consumer Goes Shopping

I need a part for my latest project, so we head out to the store.

(1) The sign says "Stock Up and Save," and I am doomed. The provident Natalie shows restraint because she has great strength of character and because she knows what we need and do not need. Grocery inventory-control software, inherited from a hundred generations of Italian women, is coded into her DNA.

I, however, purchase the promotional six-pack of work gloves because (a) I am as acquisitive as I was at age eight and (b) I have forgotten about the two promotional six-packs of gloves at home on my workbench, stacked next to the three identical boxes of sheetrock screws. And how much is that ten-pack of electrical tape?

(2) Like every woman, Natalie can return merchandise to a store without the slightest remorse. But I just hate to: it feels like a divorce.

(3) And, like every woman, she is devoted to sales. But I worry: if every item in my cart is a sale item, 50% off, how will the store stay in business?

(4) A single ¼ " x 28 x 1½ " bolt remains in the bin. I need one, but who am I? Maybe someone will run to the store tonight, desperately trying to beat the closing time, and he needs just one ¼ " x 28 x 1½" bolt to repair something more important.

Natalie knows precisely what I'm thinking and pauses to let me contemplate. After a decent interval, she offers a suggestion: Take it already and let's go.

(5) I once had a repair shop where I fixed radios and phonographs. It taught me that a store, even a huge one like this, is like someone's house. You can always recognize the store customer who once minded a store himself: he rescues merchandise that has fallen to the floor. He says goodbye when he leaves, and teaches his kids to do the same.

(6) There is a garage sale down the street. Someone's parents are gone, to the nursing home or beyond, and their lives are laid out in boxes on an aluminum table beneath an awning. There are worn tools (how did he bend that screwdriver?) and jars of nuts and bolts saved from fifty years of household repairs; guys do *not* throw away nuts and bolts. Here is her sewing machine and scraps of cloth, and his bowling ball, in its case with the shoes. The paint-by-number picture she painted, in the frame he made for her. His hi-fi speakers, stacked atop her Ladies Home Journal and his Popular Mechanics Do-It-Yourself Encyclopedia. They are traveling light for their trip into the next world, and need none of it.

I wonder if I could use that wrench.

(7) Home: we pull into the garage, where unused tools, still in their bubble packs, hang on the walls. Unfinished projects are stacked in piles, and unstarted projects are still filed in my head. I'll bet they all stand around at night, laughing at me.

Or maybe not. Perhaps the unopened, unfinished, and unstarted are content that each was briefly at the center of my attention. Perhaps they know that my intentions were good.

I'm older now, and I know that I will never finish. But maybe after my earthly self wears out the rest of me will find a place where I can use all those tools, and complete all those projects. Sort of a Garage of the Lord, where I can dwell in happiness and peace, and Natalie will call me in for dinner each evening.

Just Sign on the Dotted Line: How I Learned High Finance in Elementary School

I'm glad that the lady at the bank was patient with me when we presented ourselves to open an IRA yesterday. Natalie is fearless about these things, but I'm not: I always worry that I'll accidentally sign something in the wrong place and then find that I've just converted my assets into Panamanian savings bonds.

At least I know how I got this way. When I was a kid the lights in our house in Cleveland Heights would burn until dawn every night for the first two weeks of April while my father did the family income tax. There were explosions of rage, bitter recriminations between my parents about penalties, and long, strictly-enforced silences. My sister and I were sensible children, so we hid.

My mother told me the whole story not long ago. She said that our taxes back then were neither costly nor complicated; the problem was my father, who kept trying to invent tax shelters. It never worked, and then he'd be afraid of what the IRS might do.

My sister didn't improve my self-confidence in money matters, either. She would lovingly detail the many ways that someone—say, a little brother of borderline competence—could get into serious trouble with the law. For example, if his handwriting was really bad, he wouldn't be able to sign his name at the bank exactly the same way every time, and then he'd go to jail.

I shouldn't have listened, because fifth-graders aren't usually asked to endorse negotiable instruments. But my grandparents, who were avid investors in their retirement, had just given me two shares of General Motors stock in the faint hope that their spendthrift grandson would decide that equity ownership was really keen.

Trouble began when the first dividend check came. It was made out to Mr. Mark R. Kinsler (age 10) in the amount of something like forty cents. When I asked my father what I should do, he growled that it was high time I learned to manage things for myself.

So I signed the back of the check ("Mr. Mark R. Kinsler," in my ten-year-old's handwriting) and mailed it to the bank where I had a savings account (Balance: $18.56.) The bank graciously responded with a letter to my parents saying that I was too young to sign anything and that under the provisions of the Ohio Uniform Gifts to Minors Act I had messed things up. So I got yelled at.

After that, I tried hiding the checks when they came. But this really irritated GM's bank in New York, which sent another unpleasant letter to my parents telling them that GM Common Stock Dividend Checks #11705 through #11707 had not been cashed and that this was somehow paralyzing their accounting system. So I got yelled at again.

It took years for everything to get sorted out: apparently GM hadn't known I was just a kid because my grandparents never told them.

So for years I stayed clear of any financial document more complex than a money order. After I left college and it came time to file my first income tax return, I thought about my father and those long spring nights back home in Cleveland Heights. Accordingly, I gathered my records, marched over to the tax preparation office across the street, and told the fellow to do whatever needed to be done for whatever he and the US Government wanted me to pay. It was a liberating experience.

The other day I found my big green-and-white GM stock certificate with its engravings of 1940's cars, trucks, and locomotives. I'm looking for a frame for it.

The Father, the Son, the Land, and the Gravely Tractor.

In retrospect, my father was a brave man. I don't think I ever would have built a suburban house when I was 41, and I certainly wouldn't have thrown myself into the endless landscaping as he did. David M Kinsler: scholar, intellectual, writer. But a tiller of the soil? No. But he bought the Gravely tractor, Model L1, and struggled with it all the years we lived there.

You didn't ride on a garden tractor in 1956. It had two wheels and you walked behind it, manhandling two long handles made of one-inch iron pipe to steer the thing. You were always instructed to keep your hand on the reverse lever when you backed up because the machine was perfectly capable of running you over and killing you.

The Gravely had a one-cylinder, five-horsepower engine, but that cylinder was the size of an oatmeal box and those horses were the kind that Amish farmers pull their plows with. Dad started the machine by wrapping a three-foot leather strap around a huge iron pulley down between the handles. Make sure the gas is turned on, fool with the choke, move the throttle handle halfway down, and give that strap a pull that only a Depression kid born on the south side of Chicago in 1915 could give.

Unlike today's garden tractors, the Gravely was not designed around a lawnmower. Each of the 'accessories' —we had the Rotary Plow, the Plow Blade, and the Sickle Bar Mower— were bolted onto the front of the machine as needed, requiring that the Operator hold the tractor steady while his young son tried frantically to push four 5/8" bolts through misaligned holes.

The Rotary Plow was—well, hard to describe. It had a pumpkin-sized gearbox that stuck out from the front of the tractor, supported by two iron wheels in front. This gearbox rotated a ponderous blade that looked like a great steel boat propeller. You'd lower the boat propeller down so its blades rested on the ground and then yell at a ten-year-old Mark to "throw in the clutch!" at which fearful order I would gingerly grab a little lever to engage a pair of chattering gears. The blades would start to drill down into the earth and, when the

Operator started the tractor moving forward, they'd sort of drill sideways as they were pushed along. This unlikely arrangement could pulverize the miserable clay soil of Cleveland Heights, uprooting rocks too heavy for me to drag away.

We had an embankment that sloped 45 degrees down to the street, and I'm sure that if my father had thought about it first he probably wouldn't have tried to plow it crosswise. He did okay until the Rotary Plow hit a rock. I watched, riveted, as tractor, father, and Rotary Plow executed two complete revolutions, tumbling down the slope together. All landed upright, and my father just stood there, blinking. In the silence that followed I did not know what to say. "Boy, that thing sure is powerful," was all I could manage. This, at least, was one occasion where I thought he was justified in trying to kill me.

The Plow Blade was made of quarter-inch boiler plate. I couldn't move it, but at least it didn't need the clutch. We used it to move the huge hunks of Berea sandstone that littered the property, and to clear snow: endless snow. Glen Allen Drive runs down a hillside that faces Lake Erie, and the snowstorm that howled through northeast Ohio the night my sister graduated high school (she was a mid-termer) blew four-foot drifts across our long, sloping driveway. Occasional white flames shot six inches from the Gravely's muffler as we pushed the drifts into the street. With its tire chains installed, there was nothing that machine could not move.

The Sickle Bar Mower was simply terrifying. Consider a four-foot wide set of hair clippers, its multitude of teeth set three inches apart behind a row of foot-long spikes that funneled the grass into the rattling blades. We used it to cut heavy field grass in the big lot we owned. The Sickle Bar Mower cut heavy brush, thickets of poison ivy, and a couple of recently-planted young trees my father couldn't maneuver around in time.

I never found out what happened to the Gravely. My parents divorced, the house was sold, and the property broken up into three lots. Gravely tractors are still being made, but they now have seats, steering wheels, and electric starter.

Woman Spares Determined Boater's Life

It seemed reasonable enough. In 1975 I was living near the seashore in New Haven, Connecticut, and the bright yellow "K-Craft" four-man inflatable boat was on clearance at the local K-mart. It was seven feet long, sort of pointed at one end, and it had these plastic loops on the sides for the oars. My long-suffering companion Marilyn looked upon the transaction with the doubt that comes of long experience.

I inflated it with a series of ineffective pumps and a lot of lung exercise, tied it to the top of Marilyn's Datsun and we drove to the beach, where we discovered that you can't launch a boat without getting wet. Freed of land's embrace, the noble vessel undulated over the waves; it felt like we had gone to sea aboard a rubber raincoat.

I tried rowing, but the boat just sort of drifted. Marilyn complained we looked like shipwreck survivors and that people in other boats were watching us. I rowed faster: we went sideways. When concerned fellow boaters offered to rescue us for the third time she announced that she'd had enough.

Okay, so the problem was motive power. But even if you have a motor, which I didn't, mounting one on a rubber raft is like putting ice skates on your galoshes. So M Kinsler, naval propulsion specialist, built a pair of hand-cranked wooden paddlewheels mounted on each end of a pipe threaded through the oar loops. The finished craft looked like Robert Fulton's first steamboat. Marilyn said nothing.

To avoid further embarrassment, initial sea trials were conducted in what I assumed was a calm river nearby. We plopped the boat in, attached the paddlewheels and set off. We thrashed across to the other bank and then back again. It worked!

Only I failed to notice that the car was shrinking in the distance, and that we were now drifting down the river. I cranked the paddles, but the current was too strong.

Science note: 'Tidal rivers' reverse direction every time the tide goes in or out. The flow ceases completely during the brief period between the tides, and if you are from Cleveland Heights and think that rivers flow constantly and unendingly to the sea, except maybe in Leviticus, you can be misled. The tide was going out, and we were moving with it.

There was a bridge ahead and I grabbed onto it as we swept underneath, which would have been great if the boat hadn't started to leave without me. Given the choice of (1) spending the afternoon hanging from the middle of a bridge five feet above the river or (2) dropping back into the boat with Marilyn, I hastily chose the latter. The good ship K-craft moved ever faster, rotating majestically as we floated helplessly down to the sea.

The owner of the small wooden dock that stopped us was infinitely polite as he fished us out. His two sons came out to salvage our boat, and the paddlewheels. "Yep," he said, "that current can go 25 mph through this part of the river." Marilyn glared at me as I have seldom been glared at before or since, and I quickly set off to get the car. But I knew she would forgive me.

We parted long ago, but we are still friends. When she met Natalie some years back the two women immediately bonded, discussing me and my schemes with more laughter than I believe was warranted.

The K-craft made its final voyage to Goodwill Industries after spending years on various shelves in its box. But I could redesign those paddlewheels: I'd make extensions for the blades, first, and...

My Oldest Friend Lives Here

"Welcome to the East Mulberry Street Museum of Transportation. Please stay within the marked pathways; the natural formations of bike and auto parts have become unstable over the years."

"Foremost among the working artifacts in our collection is the 1956 Schwinn Racer, purchased new at the Taylor Road Bicycle Shop in Cleveland Heights when Mr Kinsler was nine years old. The piece was moved to its new location in the truck to aid pedestrian traffic on the back porch."

The metallic red finish has faded to a reddish brown. The seat, maybe the fifth one, is cracked and the pedals I installed during my first attempt at graduate school in 1980 are worn and slippery.

The pedal crank is rusted, and it isn't the original one anyway because the original one broke in half one afternoon and deposited the middle-aged rider onto the surface of State Route 12 near Ackerman, Mississippi during what was intended to be a health-restoring ride. Natalie had to drive the Buick out to recover the remains.

The original handlegrips said "Schwinn" on them, but they never fit quite right and I replaced them with a set of anonymous black ones. It looks like I used my father's wire cutters to trim them down.

The handlebars aren't quite even, and there's a kink in the tubing. I was showing off—to no audience at all, as twelve-year-old boys will—when I hit a patch of gravel on Hollister Street, and I never got them straightened quite right. I tried to be cool for a while with a pair of "dropped" racing handlebars, and then I bolted on the old bent ones for good.

Those aren't the original wheels, either. When I went to the bike store for a 26-inch Schwinn Tubular Rim Lightweight tire in 1989 they told me that they didn't sell antiques. With regret I bought fancy new alloy rims and built new wheels on the old hubs. I still have the old rims, bent and scraped from the curbs and potholes of nine cities, and I use the fifty-year-old spokes to build science demonstrations.

The rear fender rattles because when I was 14 I broke off its mounting tab trying to emulate a racing bike I saw by removing the fenders and thus their excess weight. It didn't help much because the *Racer*, Schwinn's concept of a lightweight bicycle in the 1950's, weighs about forty pounds with or without the fenders. I put them back on after I discovered why bicycle racers don't ride through puddles.

The frame is too small. It fit me when I was nine, and nobody thought I'd still be riding a bike at 17, so I had to install extra-long posts for the seat and handlebars. It made my bike look like a two-wheeled pogo stick, but my social life in high school couldn't have been worse anyway if I'd ridden in on my sister's roller skates.

And there you have it, museum guests: a bicycle that has rolled through an entire life. The Schwinn that took a ten-year-old to fifth grade at Noble Elementary School took an old guy up to the medical lab for a PSA blood test last week. My bike and I have aged together, and not always so gracefully. We share the same sort of scrapes and scars: it got new front brakes, I got new front teeth. It has had as many seats as I've had careers, and none of them have fit all that well. But it also took me to spelling bees and dissertation defenses, and to my first date with Natalie.

It is not for sale, thanks.

Disturbed Cat Finds New Hope at East Mulberry Street Facility

She weighs 6.8 pounds, principally stripes, fluff, and attitude. Pacing deliberately past my chair, she pauses, turns her Indian-striped face to me, utters a meow of disapproval and stalks off, flourishing a long, feathery tail in the air by way of emphasis.

She came from a semi-official shelter, a large split-level home that turned out to be a zoo with a house-like shell. Cages of abandoned cats and dogs were stacked in the living room, tamer creatures teemed underfoot. Four automatic electric cat boxes ground away in the dining room, continuously sifting treasures from the litter.

The kittens came up from the basement in a laundry basket with their mother, a serene black-and-white child bride not much larger than her little ones. Our choice was made for us when the smallest, a hauntingly-beautiful tabby with elaborate markings, fell asleep in Natalie's lap.

Her name was Pee Wee, quickly changed to Amanda. At the vet's office everyone wanted to hold her, and we handed the tiny thing around until she reminded us that she was a living creature who had only recently had lunch.

She was and is her own cat. When she attacked the stitches from her spaying operation, I had to cut the toe off an old athletic sock and pull it over the entire kitten to create a protective cylinder with cat parts—head, tail, legs—protruding from each end.

She grew up, as beautiful a cat as God ever made, until—until we saw that fur was missing from her legs and tail and underside. Off to the veterinarian, to check for fleas, allergies, disease. No: she was 'overgrooming,' obsessively cleaning herself until the fur was chewed off, and the clinical cause for this was that she was crazy.

It's bad enough getting any sort of pills into a cat, but with psychoactives you need a court order and the sheriff's department. She is stronger and smarter than the two of us, and she can hide, spit out, and otherwise elude the soothing chemicals more skillfully than we can think of ways to apply them. The cat treat does not exist that will disguise the taste or smell of powdered cat tranquilizer. The fancy canned food was a failure. The tuna didn't work, either, though Natalie made me sandwiches from the remainder of the can. We never got around to the sardines, and I forget just what it was that I tried with the maple syrup except that it seemed like a good idea at the time.

We got a mysterious jar of cat pheromones that screws into a special electric heater which plugs into an electrical outlet upstairs and vaporizes the chemicals into a cloud of kitty joy warranted to render the most disturbed feline serene and content. We breathe more of the stuff than the cat does, but it hasn't helped us, either.

The whole business is beginning to resemble one of those medical stories in the Reader's Digest with "Miracle" somewhere in the title. The latest magic bullet is the old-time tranquilizer Valium, professionally compounded into tuna-flavored cat chews and administered by Natalie each morning and evening on a small plastic platter in the bathroom sink. They seem to be helping a bit.

A lot of trouble, and I have occasionally suggested that Amanda the Cat could better serve as the lining for a pair of gloves. But I know better: Natalie loves her, and that settles it.

And I am glad. For I have many neuroses, and have neither stripes nor an appealing face. Yet Natalie says she loves me, too.

Wildflowers Say No to Captivity in Back Yard

I always wanted to grow wildflowers.

They're tough, showy and determined. I like to roam abandoned industrial sites to see God's garden poking up amongst the old building foundations, and I wanted my own thicket of them in the back yard.

So I used to buy bulging packets of 'wildflower assortments' at the garden store. These always seemed like a great idea until I tried to follow the directions: "Space plants five inches apart."

Now, the area of a square measuring five inches on a side is 25 square inches, which when multiplied by the number of tiny seeds in your typical wildflower assortment gives us an area equal to that of a collective farm in the Ukraine. So I fudged the procedure, tilling a plot that looked reasonable and then sort of mooshing the seeds around in it. Cover, water, and hope; may the best plant win, and it was usually a clump of dandelions.

Then someone told me that wildflowers should be started in pots indoors during the winter. The luxuriant snapdragons and iris that grow in the alley behind our house don't need that, but okay.

So I bought some wildflower seeds—good ones, with the extended power train warranty--and a pair of Gro-light tubes for my shop light. I made pots out of soda cans, hung the shop light over a table in the basement, and filled the pots with a mixture of garden soil and peat moss.

Master Gardener Kinsler carefully planted 4-5 seeds in each pot, covering with ¼" of soil. I carefully watered each pot from a soda bottle, which washed the seeds out from the soil and left them floating. I poked them back into the mud, turned on the Gro-light, and left.

A few hours later I crept back down. I didn't want to wake my infants, but given the care I had lavished upon them, maybe something had sprouted.

It had not. I chuckled at my silliness; ha ha, I will be patient.

Ha, ha, indeed. Nature, typically skeptical of my plans, deliberated at length over this latest scheme. I guess a favorable verdict came in, because a couple of tiny leaves eventually poked up from the surface of the over-watered soil. More followed in neighboring pots until every pot—except two, over which I mused on life and death—sprouted tiny, optimistic seed leaves.

In due course, the seed leaves were replaced by what we gardeners call 'permanent' leaves. At least that's what we call them if horticultural terminology follows that of dentistry. The spindly plants started to reach for the light.

Now, our neighbor has a very large dog of weak intellect. She regularly escapes from their fenced-in back yard, and then stands looking puzzled until someone, occasionally me, leads her back into their yard, after which she'll try to claw her way to freedom once again.

It was on one of these occasions that I happened to look into our basement windows from the neighbor's yard and saw my wildflower farm. The pots were carefully arranged on the table in the unearthly glare of the Gro-light, and you could see a bit of green. Then my imagination took over.

Yes, Officer. They're wildflowers. I can't grow them outside. Yes, I know that there are wildflowers growing out of every curb in the city, but I want—no, they're wildflowers, really. There's no need for the DEA to come all the way out here to find out that I'm just growing zinnias. But I suppose the Joint Narcotics Task Force is familiar with my gardening abilities by now, and crossed me off their list of potential marijuana farmers years ago.

I finally transplanted the tiny shoots ('when all threat of frost has passed') to a strip of soil along our front pathway, and that was the last I saw of them. Grass grows there now.

Experts Find Kids' Play Builds Character, Confidence—In Adults

The results of a one-second glance at the school playground we passed by this morning on our way to the bank were as follows: six kids were congealing into the sort of tangle that often precedes a fight, two kids were up to something of a conspiratorial nature in a distant corner, and there was no supervisor in sight.

Natalie saw none of this, but my old playground sensors were on the job, demonstrating that they still work.

It's been years since I was a substitute teacher, but once you've pulled playground duty for more than a week you will never thereafter walk past a playground without watching for coats left on the fence or kids escaping the penalty area against the wall. You'll always know the difference between a make-believe shriek and a real one, and you can compute the range and bearing of the latter within milliseconds.

It was never boring. Most schools don't have nurses anymore, and the medical procedures improvised in school offices would do justice to an Army field hospital. Case history: A small girl was brought in from the field of honor after stopping a basketball with her face. Something had snapped in her braces, and it was hurting her mouth badly enough to bring tears.

My sister is a dentist, and I am not, but I had her open up anyway. I lucked out: I could see the piece of wire that was digging into the poor kid's gum, and I could reach it. The American Dental Association wouldn't approve, but the small screwdriver I always carry proved just adequate to pry the wire away from the gum. We packed it with a bit of Kleenex to stop the bleeding, and within five minutes our invalid had bounded back outside to join her friends.

I'm still amazed at how tough kids can be. We elders look up at the monkey bars we once scrambled over with disbelief: how could anyone survive a fall off those? Shouldn't there be railings, or safety harnesses, or mattresses to line the area?

But the kids are blessed with the knowledge that they're constructed of space-age plastics that bounce off unyielding surfaces without damage. They jump right off, again and again, head first if you're not looking.

Case history #2: One afternoon at a rural Ohio school I learned that kids can withstand power surges that'll blow the memory out of a military-grade microprocessor. The playground there had an elaborate spiral-shaped slide made of bright red and blue plastic. The kids would climb the ladder and with a shriek of joy disappear into a curved tunnel, to emerge laughing at the bottom.

As I cleared out the third traffic pile-up in the tunnel I heard a crackling. It was electricity: the kids' nylon jackets were rubbing static electric charge off that plastic spiral, raising their individual kid voltages into the thousands.

One tiny girl, her blonde hair standing straight out from her slippery pink nylon parka, shot from the bottom of the slide into my arms. The electric arc that snapped from her nose to my hand was memorable. At least I remember it; it hurt. But she laughed and scampered back up the ladder.

That was about five years ago. I still instinctively scan every playground I pass, and I want to stop and help if there's a fight or an accident. But it's almost unlawful for a man to go near a playground now. So I walk on, hoping that the supervisor on duty has developed her playground antennas as well as I once did.

The Kinslers and the Automotive Circle of Life

Our first family car was a dark-green dirigible of a 1949 Oldsmobile 98 with a Rocket V-8 engine, a Hydramatic transmission, and green plaid seats. And by 1958 it was pretty well shot: Vera G Kinsler and the noble barge had become regulars at Sears Auto Repair on Carnegie Avenue, and she began to call it the Searsmobile. The Olds' fate was sealed one cold winter day when, while waiting for the light at 55th and Euclid, the engine fell out.

So the Kinsler family went car shopping. The first invasion of foreign cars had just reached Cleveland, and my father liked the concept. So we looked at the NSU Prinz and the Borgward Isabella. We test drove the Simca and the Renault Dauphine; the DKW and the Vauxhall. And the Volkswagen, which for the 1959 model year had been updated with a rear window you could see out of.

The VW salesman enthusiastically demonstrated the tight steering and the emergency brake, making the two kids hanging onto each other in the back seat wish that someone would invent seat belts already. My father was impressed, and a few days later we proudly drove home in a crisp new 1959 Volkswagen, beige. Available options included an outside mirror and a radio: we got the mirror.

Volkswagen was a cult in the 1950's. There were Volkswagen clubs, and VW drivers honked at each other as they passed. My father really got into it, wearing one of those flat English tweed caps and lecturing us on the finer techniques of the stick shift while the 36-horsepower engine roared its little heart out.

We took it on New England vacation trips, and out to rural Ohio. My mother taught me and my sister to drive in it. My father built an exquisite car-top carrier from strips of varnished oak, testing it out by stacking up four bales of straw for our compost pile and driving them home from the farm store.

But Cleveland lies downwind of Lake Erie, and it snows all winter. The city tried every method to melt the pack ice from the streets, including an unfortunate experiment with a jet engine mounted on a truck. But nothing really worked except road salt, and our police patrolled in cruisers with no rocker panels. The Volkswagen got good gas economy because it was light, and it was light because it was welded out of thin steel sheets, and the salt on Mayfield Road ate it like a Hostess cupcake.

The VW was five years old when my parents brought home a blue '64 Chevrolet Biscayne with an in-line six-cylinder engine and a three-speed stick shift, yet another exciting car for the teenagers. We kept the Volkswagen for a father-and-son restoration project my father proposed on the theory that this would somehow preserve both the car and our relationship. Time has mercifully dimmed the memory of those grim hours in the garage, but the little car continued to run.

I never found out what happened to it, or the Biscayne for that matter. Both were gone when I came home on a brief college break, and I made no comment on the Chrysler convertible in the driveway.

And that's why auto body rust is a personal issue, to be rooted out and eliminated with a zeal worthy of the Old Testament whenever I find it. Natalie wisely stays clear, intervening only at day's end to tell me what nobody in Cleveland ever did: that her love will endure any degree of corrosion damage to the car, or even to me.

Making New Friends on East Mulberry Street

Natalie just called me outside to meet a visitor. The introduction was made on our front railing, currently decorated and much enhanced by a fortunate tangle of morning glory. My beloved had laid her hand thereupon and felt a couple of sharp pokes, as if from thorns. This is odd, because of all the problems presented by that contradictory plant, thorns are not on the list.

So Natalie looked down and there, glaring back at her with considerable annoyance, was a small praying mantis. We admired her at length, but she was more concerned with getting on with her business and also not being crushed by people who should be getting on with theirs.

She is a smallish specimen, and brownish grey, though Natalie says that our new friend displayed some green when she spread her wings. My guess is that Ms Mantis changed to her autumn wardrobe about the same time Natalie did, placing her summer costume of dark green into storage next to the brighter green ensembles of spring.

The outraged insect regarded us carefully, turning her wise triangular head this way and that. She did not flee, and it occurs to me that she might be surveying our railing, which is in a fashionable location and has a hollow space in the upper curlicue suitable for an egg case; Ms Mantis was inspecting just this spot when Natalie poked a hand into her life. We hope she stays, and resolve to keep our mitts well away from her real estate.

The other insect residents of our ancient plot include a cloud of gnats who, for reasons best known to their executive council, have occupied the same airspace near the rear garage door for the last four seasons. And this year we have a multitude of crickets of every size and variety, ready to scuttle out to scare the daylights out of us.

At Natalie's direction I have rescued several. "Someone is swimming laps in here," she announced one day last week. "Would you like to rescue him?" We were washing a crop of tomatoes and found a minute cricket, caught up in the harvest operation, treading water in the kitchen sink. The US Coast Guard Search and Rescue Service made the pickup with a cupped hand and released him onto the back stoop. Natalie called a warning for him to beware of hungry birds.

And there was a sighting of—well, perhaps the strangest insect I have ever seen. One afternoon I was doing some long-deferred weeding and on some leaf litter in the garden near the beans saw a yellow glint. Lying in a curled leaf was a bright golden bead, perhaps one of the gold ball earrings Natalie wears. Then the gold ball earring unfolded its wings and hopped over to the next leaf. Then it folded itself up to become a gold bead once again. Upon further reflection I determined that my mind had finally taken the southbound 3:10 freight to Atlanta, but the Internet disagreed: I had beheld a Golden Tortoise Beetle (*Metriona bicolor).*

In a house as old as ours one can expect to host occasional insect guests of varying visual appeal. I have long learned to recognize the particular cry signifying the presence of an arthropod in the bathtub, upon which I grab my trusty margarine tub and cardboard sheet and head upstairs. Trapping the target beneath the yellow container, I slide the cardboard beneath bug and tub, lifting all three out of the tub, downstairs and out the door to freedom.

It's the decent thing to do: they lived here before we did.

Attention, Customers: Live Broadcast From Aisle Eight, By the Canned Tuna

When I was about nine my favorite radio announcer Wes Hopkins did a remote broadcast at a new drugstore in Cleveland, and I somehow got my mother to take me there. I loved radio, and fifteen years later in 1971 I was excited when my employer, WTSO-AM of Madison WI, ruled that part of my new job would be to work on remote broadcasts.

We would go out to someone's store and build a complete little studio inside, with a desk, microphone, turntable and miles of wire, and then spend the day running the radio station from there. The announcer would talk, and I would play the records.

People were supposed to get excited about this and come in and buy things. But customers in Wisconsin don't get very excited, and once they determined that we were not sale merchandise they would gaze at us sorrowfully and move on.

We got more attention the day we set up in a hardware store. Our table was blocking one of the racks, and so while the Lettermen sang, we spent the morning matching and dispensing vacuum cleaner belts. Hoover topped the charts, but Eureka was climbing fast with their latest hit, the 52100B (fits all uprights.)

To aid sagging sales we endured five consecutive days in the atrium of West Towne Mall, 9 a.m. to 9 p.m., six feet in front of the loudest decorative fountain in North America. To this day I can lip sync every selection from that playlist with perfect accuracy.

And then there was the environmental movement. One sunny July morning we set up in the parking lot of a large supermarket, there to celebrate Coca Cola's new can recycling program. Bring in clean aluminum cans, and get a prize. Save the Earth.

It was an adventure for all the senses. Whenever the DJ switched on his microphone to announce the time, temperature, and the call letters of our unfortunate station, another load of cans would thunder into a nearby truck. Those that missed rolled and clattered at our feet.

As the day wore on it became apparent that further education would be required before the general public truly understood the difference between clean recyclables and fried chicken remnants long past their due date. People would pull up in a station wagon, claim their prize, and into the truck would sail a sack containing a week's worth of aromatic household refuse. Our fan base consisted largely of flies.

We soldiered on, a sweltering musical dot in a flat sea of trash-strewn, sun-baked blacktop, playing sprightly tunes to an unseen audience. Driven more by the relentless continuity that governs life at any broadcast facility than by any desire to be further employed at one, I put the needle on the next record, a seven-inch 45 rpm disk, and started it up.

It didn't sound much like "Rainy Days and Mondays." We looked: the record was somehow off-center on the turntable and the arm was weaving back and forth, trying to follow the grooves. The DJ, a professional, instantly cut in with the next commercial.

Noted surrealist artist Salvador Dali came to mind when I picked up the record to see what was wrong, for the black disk flopped over my hand like a fried egg. The turntable, blistering hot from the sun, had melted it. The next record in the stack had not yet reached the fluid state, so I stuck it on the turntable and signed to the DJ to hurry up already before that one melted, too.

The prevailing opinion back at the radio station was that this couldn't have happened to anyone but me.

It Eats Grass But Has the Heart Of A Lion

It looks like Lazarus the Lawnmower will be with us for another season. After this year's oil change, which yielded a can of viscous black goo mixed with antique grass clippings, I gave the engine a precision tune-up consisting primarily of a can of old-style flammable carburetor cleaner sprayed into every orifice. It started on the second pull.

I'd never had a power mower before we moved here. David M Kinsler was a firm believer in the healthful benefits of hand mowing, and I guess I am too. Our antique-collecting neighbors from Athens gave us a hand mower on permanent loan so I could carry on the tradition, but our lawn was cut out of someone's sorghum field in maybe 1913 and that grass is tough. So four years ago, exhausted and no longer sixteen, I began my search for some mechanical assistance.

Compared to that hand mower, just about anything would do, and that's pretty much what I got: a red push-type rotary mower with a fatally-bent crankshaft, the result of an altercation with a concrete hammock base. Free. The repair tag on the handle said "DUMPSTER."

Contrary to local folklore, you cannot straighten a crankshaft by striking it several sharp blows with a sledge hammer and a two-by-four. Natalie wisely hid while I beat the daylights out of the poor thing for half a day.

It had to come apart. My little Harbor Freight hydraulic press once again proved its worth as it shoved the bent shaft out through the lower main bearing. For some reason nothing broke, and with the crankshaft out, I was able to straighten it so it didn't wobble all that badly. Craftsmanship is our watchword here at Kinsler Engine Works.

The damage from the initial beating wasn't too bad, and I finally got the flywheel on correctly. I gave the starter cord a pull, and with a mighty roar Lazarus the Lawnmower rose from the dead in a cloud of burning oil.

Of course, there were modifications. The throttle control, with its international symbols showing the turtle (slow) and the rabbit (fast) was troublesome, so I removed it and wired the throttle wide open. The automatic blade brake quickly followed, though this eliminated any means of stopping the engine except by shorting out the spark plug with a shovel.

The vertical-shaft Briggs and Stratton engine may be the most reviled piece of machinery on Earth, but Lazarus is a champ. Bursting with pride, I called the lawnmower place to tell them that I'd fixed their machine, and thank you, and wasn't I great.

They were horrified. It turns out they lived in fear that the crankshaft would break off and then the blade would somehow find its way out from under the mower housing and go spinning down the block, beheading children on its way. This seemed to me to be a bit far-fetched, although the machine once sailed a rock into the neighbor's yard and left a substantial dent in the side of his charcoal grill.

When the gas tank fell apart two years ago I redesigned the bracket and sealed it up with epoxy glue. And when last year the engine started stalling, I took the cover off to find that the ignition module had lost a screw and was swinging merrily on the remaining one, occasionally sending current to the spark plug whenever it happened to be near the flywheel.

Together, we will keep the lawn cut this summer. Lazarus still wears the "DUMPSTER" tag to remind us that there is always hope, even for the least of God's children.

Lancaster Resident Witnesses Decades of Progress in Dentistry

Maybe if the City of Cleveland had started fluoridating its water before my permanent teeth grew in I might not have spent so much of my life staring up at acoustical-tile ceilings with my mouth pried open. Over the course of years I have read, in installments, the entire run of the Large-Print Edition of the Readers' Digest prior to settling into the Chair of Regret and opening up. I have explored, in detail, the nostrils of three generations of dentists.

It didn't help that the young Kinsler was inexplicably opposed to brushing his teeth. It also didn't help that my mother insisted that baking soda was a perfectly adequate dentifrice; I probably could have used Crest to good advantage. But the patient Dr. Max D. Hoffman, DDS, said no, that my teeth were soft and decay-prone anyway. And so I have spent years learning to distinguish fine vintages of Novocain.

What really fixed me up was my moped, which is a sort of heavy bicycle with a little engine. I bought one from a kid for ninety-five bucks and proceeded not long afterwards to sail it into the side of an Oldsmobile. They repaired the bike and my teeth, but the bike came out better. It got a new front fork and I got a root canal and a double crown over my two front teeth.

I really can't complain. That rig lasted for 37 years, right up to a couple of years ago when I bit into a Tootsie Roll stolen from our Halloween basket and a tooth crumbled. Verdict: I would need a dental implant.

Now, implants are great because they're strong, like real teeth. But they're screwed right into your jawbone, and the condition of my particular jawbone was such that the procedure would have been like threading a half-inch lag screw into a sheetrock wall.

It took months to build up the socket with artificial bone, during which time I got to wear a dental plate with a single tooth in it so I wouldn't look like Hoss on Bonanza and whistle each word in my physics lectures.

Of course, the plate was far too delicate to eat with. Even a donut would break it, and I took to keeping bottles of Crazy Glue handy for emergency repairs. I learned to not do this in the car because if you try to hold the parts together while gluing them you get an anatomically-interesting sculpture consisting of three fingers and a front tooth.

Finally my jawbone was certifiably sturdy. He drilled a hole right into the new bone and expanded it out with a hammer and punch, like he was removing a dent from a shotgun barrel.

And then he screwed in the implant. With a wrench. A wrench with a ratchet on it, like they sell at Sears. I felt like every engine I ever screwed a spark plug into.

The new tooth was just great, but it felt strange at first. That's because natural teeth are anchored flexibly in their sockets, but the implant was set rigidly in my upper jaw, which made it feel like I was biting into an apple with my forehead.

I didn't care. I could once again eat an ear of corn without leaving a median strip, and I laid the dental plate away as a trophy.

Everything went splendidly in the fang division for months, until the night I bit into a piece of Italian bread and with a *crunch* the next tooth over broke off. The American Dental Association has promised me a monogrammed bib with a gold chain.

Place the Following in Their Proper Order: (a) AARP card (b) First Piano Lesson.

The Bible seems to have left out the Parable of the Elderly Piano Student, and how he learned the true meaning of humility.

My musical education started off with cello lessons at age 12. It was a swell experience: the teacher yelled at me, the school orchestra director yelled at me and, and my father dreamed—and apparently believed—that I would soon play in the Cleveland Orchestra. Mine was a common story in Cleveland Heights, which is probably why no famous musicians come from there.

I stuck with the cello for years. But what I really wanted was to play the piano: show tunes, country, and other cheerful, popular music. With a cello, there's only classical music, and even then you have to be in an orchestra or be content with a solo repertoire that seems to consist entirely of 19th-century German laments.

In college I bought a teach-yourself piano book and sat down at one of Ohio State's big old Hamilton upright pianos, ready to learn. A stalwart lad, I gave up within two weeks.

My cello experience didn't help much. I could play it, but only one note at a time. You play a piano with both hands at once, and there are big black chords that lie across the staff like a highway barrier.

Besides, I couldn't afford a piano anyway.

But one night a couple of years ago I saw a big electronic keyboard at the Radio Shack outlet. It had suffered a confrontation with a fork lift truck, but it played. Ninety bucks.

Without knowing quite why, I bought it and took it home. For a couple of weeks I poked around on the keys. I thought about buying a piano-teaching computer program.

My boss Becky sniffed at this and arranged with Phillipa, our school's young music professor, to make me take real piano lessons. After a short interview I was sent off to buy Book 1 of *Piano Adventures* and issued orders to present myself the following Tuesday.

That was two years ago, and I'm working through Book 5. Kids who could be my great-grandchildren have gone through Book 18, if there is one. But I have loved it, and nobody has yelled at me even once, though Phillipa sometimes looks ready to grind my bones to bake her bread.

Today, for example, she discovered that I had clandestinely penciled some code marks I invented onto the music because my wits aren't nimble enough to interpret music notation without expending some effort.

Erase it all, she commanded. When I played the pieces again they were better.

But progress is slow when you're old. The regrets of an ill-spent life flash through my mind whenever we begin a lesson. Sometimes the neurotransmitters in charge of survival receive a Code Red from the cortex and commence shutdown procedures, and I stare at the music like the notes have just sprouted legs and danced off the page.

It wouldn't hurt if I practiced more, and if I didn't get distracted when I do. The piano has brought back every poor study habit I ever had. Phillipa forgives each backslide with the patience of a saint, and pushes me onward. There is hope for Book Six.

And maybe there will be more help. A year ago I bought a huge old Hamilton upright piano. I noticed that it was much like the one I tried in college, so I asked the dealer where it might have come from.

I believe that there may be an old friend out there in our living room. My piano, he said, was from Ohio State University.

Raised in Luxury, a New Generation of Birds Spurns Traditional Housing

It was to be a bird community with tradition and character: all-natural birdhouse units in an all-natural environment. I never did get around to naming it—"The Estates at East Mulberry" would have been good—but anyway it's gone now, yet another avian real-estate failure.

I was fascinated when I first learned about the birdhouse squash, Lagenaria siceraria. It's a big gourd that grows on a vine, and after it dries out you can use it for a bottle, a scoop, an Indian rattle or, if you drill a hole for a doorway, a birdhouse. So I decided that I would grow some and build bird condominiums.

They were easy to grow. The vines took over the garden fence, grabbed onto the electric meter, hoisted themselves up the TV cable feed, grew out onto the telephone lines and by the time I tore them down to paint the house they were fighting it out for supremacy with the electric lines. Big squat green squash the size of bowling balls grew everywhere. I guessed that the Indians just let them dry out over the winter, so that's what I did, and by spring I had collection of hollow brownish gourds that rattled.

Construction began on the Estates. I'd read somewhere that the entryway should be one inch in diameter, so I took my one-inch spade bit, chucked it into the electric drill and upon applying it to a likely gourd watched the future Apartment One shatter into all-natural pieces all over the garage. I learned to take it easy on the remaining ten.

Now, good real-estate planning requires a careful eye for an attractive setting that's close to schools, shopping, and public transportation. I decided that our old aluminum awnings, the mounting brackets of which have supported the nests of generations of sparrows, would be suitable: I would hang one brown gourd from each awning and watch what happened.

What happened was that Natalie, acting on behalf of good taste in home décor, issued an edict directing me to establish my nesting colony somewhere else, thank you. I could have hung them from a tree if we had a tree, which we don't, so I made one out of steel electrical conduit: a big T ten feet wide and ten feet high.

The project took hours. I painted the gourds to preserve them, poked holes in the bottoms so they wouldn't accumulate water, and attached them to the crossbar of the T with nylon parachute cord.

The resulting structure looked like the Sacred Temple Bells of Tibet as I raised it into place near the garage, the hollow gourds clonking merrily back and forth on their rot-resistant cords. I secured it to our old backyard clothes pole and waited for tenants.

There weren't any. Two seasons later, there still weren't. Nobody even perched on the crossbar to inspect.

It was up there for years, looking like an offering to ancient gods of the Solomon Islands. Natalie tolerated it, as she tolerates all the rest of my nonsense, with grace and kindness. It was I who finally got sick of looking at the wretched thing and lowered it to the ground. I took off the gourds and saved the electrical conduit for another project.

I guess rustic bird villages aren't fashionable. There's a big 28-unit condo birdhouse mounted on a pole not far away, with swimming pool and health club privileges included in the rent.

Next year we'll put in a bird bath, and erect luxury waterfront gourds that won't swing in the wind. "The Dwellings at Mulberry East" sounds good.

Noted Lone Wolf Kinsler Learns How Independent He Really Is

I watch her car disappear around the corner. She's on her way to visit her sister in Pittsburgh for a week, and my presence is neither required nor requested.

I suspect a lot men react like I do when a wife leaves for more than a few hours. It's a combination of despair and irrational resentment, with some of the Call of the Wild mixed in. We're reduced to bachelorhood, something we once treasured: got along without you before I met you, gonna get along without you now.

In morose celebration of my temporary freedom, I buy food she would narrow her eyes at. Though I hear her objections at each forbidden aisle, into the cart go the five pounds of roasted peanuts, the liver sausage, the strange sugar-coated cereal and the two pound block of mild cheddar cheese. I'll show her.

Someone meows as I stow the contraband in the refrigerator. Now hear this, cats: We are stuck here without her for a week, and I'm no happier than you are. Medication will be administered as required, without negotiation. If anyone wants to go outside, go, but don't expect regular checks on your coordinates and desires. Food and water will be replenished as necessary, generally when I think of it. That is all.

They look at me: Where is she? What have you done with her?

The phone rings: "I got here. And you're making yourself sick on that stuff you bought, aren't you?"

In the morning there is nobody to share the funnies with, so the newspaper stays in its rubber band, and there is no breakfast. I hadn't eaten breakfast for twenty years the day I met her and I'm not about to fry up a stack of flapjacks now.

After all these years Natalie still expects me to prepare regular, well-balanced meals for myself, with napkin and silverware. I ignore the illustrated lecture she gave at the refrigerator—here is the frozen chili, here is the leftover cake—and eat peanut butter sandwiches over the sink.

Time to get some work done already. I turn on the radio, turn up the volume, and begin a randomly-selected project, and then another. It gets dark. She calls in at eleven from her sister's house to tell me that she's going to sleep, and that she misses me.

I get something to eat, my culinary freedom already tasting a bit stale. I visit the Internet and practice the piano, go back to the project and behold, it is 3:35 a.m. She is the only clock I ever heed: if she's in bed reading a book, it's late evening, and if she's reading the newspaper and drinking coffee, it's morning. Without the Woman of Steady Habits here to give me an idea of the time of day, I quickly slip into my traditional circadian rhythms, which resemble those of a bat.

Days go by. I'm certain we once had two cats, but one, recalling his vanished bachelorhood, has taken up permanent residence on the neighbor's porch. The other has been in hiding since I tried to administer her daily pill and sat on her tail.

More days pass. The cats are gone; maybe I'll join them. The Internet is boring: I've answered every e-mail and read every news story. What am I doing alone in this big house? What is my life's purpose?

Then there is a rattle at the door, and my life's purpose is standing there, directing me to bestir myself and unload the car. She is back, and I am complete once again.

Local Man Admits to Lassitude, Seasonal Influences Cited

It is spring, and suddenly Outside has become part of our lives again.

It is a wondrous place, especially on a warm Ohio day in early May. The oak trees I planted last fall were dead sticks, rattling against their bracing ropes in the wind all winter. Then, miraculously, there were buds, and now there are leaves. Not just leaves, but oak leaves, precisely as illustrated in the book. Such literate trees, to be able to do that.

More old friends are back: the rhubarb promises more stalks than we'll be able to consume, and the asparagus, unattended among the weeds, has grown a real asparagus stalk, shared by us at dinner last night.

The grapevines have put on new leaves. They must be pruned and braced, and I'll probably do it wrong, even though I could look up the instructions in the Book of Leviticus: he who seeks not the wisdom of the Lord is like unto the fool, woe unto him, who dwelleth in his vineyard, striving therein to build an arbor out of electrical conduit and plastic tie straps.

The kids are back. They couldn't have left for the winter like the robins, but where were they? Now, they're everywhere, on their silly pink bicycles and roller skates. Our cats stalk warily past their newly-chalked sidewalk sketches, lest unwanted admirers make improper advances.

The sparrows are back; their precarious nests once again constructed in the mounting brackets of our aluminum awnings. It looks like the grandkids have moved into 4C by the dining room, while the parents and grandparents have returned to 4A and 4B, just outside the bathroom window. The young birds are still in ground school, but the old training run from awning to fence to gutter and back to awning has been re-commissioned, and the old aviators will be flying air cover over their fluttering students by next month.

Old adversaries are back. This is the year we shall stay ahead of the weeds, I say. Ha, reply the dandelions, waiting demurely amidst the surrounding grasses.

I look away for an instant, distracted by the warm breeze, and up shoot the stalks. Yellow flowers, impossibly bright in the UV-rich light of late morning, flash out to snag the first gullible young bees that bumble past.

Thus fertilized, the blossoms snap shut, every pretense to beauty dropped, and we turn to business. In the darkness the cells swiftly key the latest software updates into the system, adding another season's lessons of survival to the DNA of a million years past. Dandelion Version 1000000.2 will savor my bottle of Round-Up like a fine Chardonnay.

And then the efficient enzymes are pumped into the seed head, and before he can stumble back from the garage with weed killer and spade, the gardener can only look on helplessly as a hundred thousand new seeds paratroop over East Mulberry Street, singing songs of the Motherland.

The tree that keeps growing out the side of our garage is back. Larger than ever, with weird-shaped leaves and the determination of the Children of Israel, it is now growing inside the garage, too. A new branch, luxuriant with vegetation, has emerged from the floor between the motor oil and the bag of charcoal.

And whoever has been living in a hole beneath our sidewalk for the last six years is back; throwing aside the soil with renewed vigor after his long winter's nap beneath the dryer vent. We don't know what he is, and I'm afraid to find out. But it is spring, and there is life and warmth enough to share with everyone.

No charges yet filed in Lancaster giblet explosion, authorities say.

I think I've got the place decontaminated by now, but Natalie wants the HazMat team to start stripping the topsoil.

What happened was that Natalie bought a whole chicken the other day, and we roasted him, and he was swell. During the preparation, she summoned me to the kitchen to show me the neat parchment bag containing the late bird's giblets. She gingerly poured its contents into a plastic refrigerator container, closed it firmly, and held it out to me. "Here," said she. "You'll probably want to do something with these."

I have always liked chicken giblets, fried or microwaved. Natalie disapproves. She also opposes beef kidney, which I also like, and has a zero-tolerance policy toward liver, or anything that looks like or might ever have looked like liver. She says that I am welcome to cook anything I want as long as I clean up after myself, but I really don't think it's worth the risk.

But when this evening we started to draw down our accrued balance of refrigerated leftovers, I retrieved the little container of giblets, popped it open and, on detecting no signs of corruption, placed it in the microwave oven.

About a minute later, I heard a pop. Nature encloses her creatures' giblets in tough membranes, and sometimes they'll explode in the microwave.

The book that came with the microwave oven was clearly written by a woman, because it says rather stiffly that exploding food is Not Funny and that every effort should be made to avoid it. But it is funny, and anyway it wasn't much of a mess, and I cleaned it up.

The giblets needed more cooking, so I put them back in. We were checking e-mail when the shot heard 'round the world came from the vicinity of the kitchen.

Forensic examination showed the gizzard had detonated. It looked like a horror movie in there, so I got the dishcloth and went to work. A giblet-laden shockwave must have blown down the waveguide into the magnetron tube, but the oven still seemed okay.

And though physically damaged and a bit raw, the giblets still smelled good, and I was hungry. Besides, there was nothing left to explode, so I put them back in the oven.

I was wrong. This chicken must have been booby-trapped by Marxists. I'm surprised the door stayed on the oven. The walls of the death chamber were again caked with chicken insides, and our whole place reeked of incinerated bird. Lying next to the overturned container was the smoking husk of a gizzard once held in high regard by both the chicken and myself.

"I'm going out for a while," announced Natalie. "I can't stand the smell." But it was dark outside, so she turned on two ceiling fans and retreated upstairs.

Again, I cleaned. There was chicken shrapnel on the door of the dishwasher, and on the cover of the mixer. I thought I'd gotten it all by the time my beloved re-appeared. The smell will disperse, I assured her.

She would have none of it. "Look at this," she cried, leveling an accusatory finger at the kitchen sink. "There are crumbs of that stuff here, and here."

"And what's this?" she demanded, stalking back to Ground Zero and pointing at three crumbs of unidentifiable organic matter lying within the much-scrubbed microwave.

Natalie says that she will have to re-sanctify our microwave oven by cooking lemon-water in it. Her friend Cathe says that I owe her a new one, and that only a man would think the incident was funny.

Local Man Discovers the Benefits of Healthful Exercise

The Pro-form 740CS is a treadmill, the latest in Natalie's vast, sequential arsenal of exercise equipment.

Her original collection included a four-foot diameter trampoline and a precarious rowing machine that inexplicably came with a bonus set of kitchen knives. Then came leg weights and arm weights, dumbbells of so many sizes that you can arrange them like a set of socket wrenches, a selection of rubber straps, and at least two exercise mats. She would have bought a step for her step aerobics, but I figured that we could save fifty bucks with a concrete block.

Then she wanted an electric treadmill. The quest took us through most of the retail space in Fairfield County, including a used sports equipment place. It was there that I found the vintage Exercycle, a stark, serious bicycle-thing from the 1950's. It looks like a rodeo bucking machine combined with a garden tiller. You sit on the little seat while a no-nonsense motor bolted to the front of the device flexes your torso back and forth and spins your feet with the pedals. Thus does the Exercycle built strength of body and mind in those able to stay alive on it. I gleefully recommended the machine to Natalie, who gave me a look.

Hooray: the treadmill of our, or at least her, dreams was on sale at Sears. I drove the old truck over to pick it up the next day.

I have hauled sacks of concrete, blocks of sandstone, logs, railroad ties, pianos, and machine tools, but none were as heavy as the Pro-form 740CS. It took two sturdy loading dock guys and me to get it into the truck, during which task I uttered several choice phrases concerning the likely lifespan of my beloved if I survived the ordeal.

"Don't ever say that," cautioned one of the loading-dock guys. "They give you a longer sentence."

I backed the truck up to our front door and levered the crate through the vestibule to the foot of our fifteen-step, 45-degree antique Lancaster staircase.

A few years ago I mounted a hand-cranked boat-trailer winch onto a heavy steel tube in the hopes that, properly anchored, it could haul an automobile out of a muddy trench. It will not. But the rig served to drag Jumbo up to Natalie's bedroom.

I propped the tube between Natalie's doorframe and the newel post atop the staircase, and fashioned a rope sling. The cats hid. I gave Natalie instructions to stay out of the way and started cranking. The crate ascended. About a third of the way up, a pretty little head peeped around the corner to assess our progress. I yelled at her to stay OUT of the way, and continued. Halfway up, the little head appeared once again, and then a rope slipped.

Natalie can move quickly when she wants to, and our old house is built like Admiral Nelson's flagship. So the only casualty was a piece of marble slab I was once going to do something with. Sheared it right in half. The Pro-form 740CS itself is indestructible.

I got a tow rope from the car and reinforced the sling. No little head appeared as I cranked Old Faithful to the top of the stairs.

The Pro-form 740CS has turned out to be quite a nice unit; Natalie likes it. Sometimes I'll hear the motor humming upstairs and little feet pounding their way to nowhere.

*A*nd when it's time to move the Pro-form 740CS once again, I will disassemble it first. With a cutting torch. `

Mother of the Year

We pull into the parking lot in Cleveland amid piles of snow that tower above Natalie's car, as if I needed yet another reminder of boyhood winters spent here. We've come to visit my mother at her 'assisted living' complex, a place she describes as a nursing home with chandeliers.

Vera G. Kinsler is as tough, smart, and unreasonable as the day she first confronted the world in 1919. Her mother was a radiant beauty who died in 1929, her father was a lawyer with a weakness for gambling, and she tells stories of the two brilliant sisters, Vera Antoinette and Sara Deane, growing up in an unstable home and blowing away the academic competition straight through college.

Her kindly, impractical father allowed the girls to stay home from high school and study on their own, going in as necessary to ace the examinations. She went to four different colleges in four years, transferring out when she got bored or when the wildly-variable family fortunes couldn't cover the costs. She landed at tuition-free Ohio State University, where she survived by ordering cases of high-end canned goods on her father's charge account from Halle's, the fanciest department store in Cleveland, cooking on the heater in her dorm room in Neil Hall. At home one summer, she used the kitchen stove to do a study of newly-discovered vitamins on plants, and a good plant biology journal published the paper she wrote.

She graduated with every honor the school could offer except the job skills necessary to survive the Great Depression. And so off she went to graduate school in Chicago, briefly funded by one of my grandfather's mysterious businesses. There she had to take a calculus course, and her university-assigned tutor, one David M Kinsler, was irretrievably snagged by her blue eyes and intellect.

"I have a limp lamp," she announces from her book-piled bed. And indeed, her long-armed bedside lamp is sagging. We sit there in her bedroom while I fix the lamp and she tells Natalie more stories. Some are true, but the fictional content is increasing.

She's been debilitated by a series of strokes over the years, proudly refusing to cooperate with anyone's efforts at physical therapy. Though the nurses say that she's finally taking all of her pills instead of hiding the ones she doesn't like, she still won't eat the food they serve, and relies on us to smuggle in candy; we figure that there are worse vices to have when you're 87. With no particular desire or talent for survival, she nonetheless survived forty years of a violent marriage, alcoholism, shock treatments, four bouts of pneumonia (the oxygen tanks stand ready in her living room) and repeatedly gripes that her body just refuses to give up.

Just to see her reaction, I ask if she's been enjoying the various activities offered by the eager staff: the sing-alongs and trips to casinos. "Look," she says. "Most of the inmates here weren't so brilliant in their prime, and being a hundred years old doesn't help anyone's intellect."

Her vision is failing, and we doubt that she's using her computer or doing much reading now, but there's no way to tell because she's still smarter than we are. She misses my sister, who has retired to California to be near her kids; Miriam cared for our impossible mother for thirty years and has earned the rest. The patient staff at her place loves her, probably for her spirit as much as anything. She fights on, a crazy, indomitable force of nature in a world not demonstrably more rational than she is.

Go get 'em, Mom.

Prehistoric Creatures Refinance Yet Another Venue.

The Bedouin herdsman, lost in the desert, relies on his camel to get him through the sandstorm. When a blizzard strikes, the Inuit hunter's faithful huskies will pull him to safety. The cowboy's horse leads him to the water hole and survival. And for the science museum, there's the dinosaur.

Three years ago the huge, tomb-like museum in Columbus was in money trouble. Matters were almost at a crisis before the administration finally obeyed their tribal instincts and ordered the biggest, cheapest, traveling dinosaur exhibit they could find fast. The one they got featured full-size plaster models of dinosaur skeletons from China, positioned in life-like poses and accompanied by Chinese dinosaur music, which uses lots of gongs.

I was new to the art and mystery of museum work, but it was clear from the condition of the crates that the science museum in Arizona where the dinosaurs had resided the previous year maintained a faith-based policy when it came to packing. The dinosaurs themselves had entered eternal rest eons ago, but the replicas of their earthly remains were rattling around in their boxes, thoroughly battered and soaked on the journey to our museum.

Museum exhibit construction is like nothing else you've ever done. I sawed out boards to replace the rotted ones in the skeleton bases. I helped sew the huge, torn murals back together, and teetered on a sixteen-foot stepladder to mount them on the gallery walls. Other workers, more expert than I, repaired fractured bones. Since these were Chinese dinosaurs we ordered a pallet of bamboo poles to build crowd barriers, and I spent days down in the shop sawing the stuff on a bandsaw, accumulating enough scrap bamboo to open a Filipino restaurant.

Every traveling museum exhibit is supposed to have people who travel with it, but the two guys from Inner Mongolia who knew how to put our skeletons together had visa problems. A few days before the heavily-advertised opening date we finally learned that they wouldn't be arriving at all, leaving us stuck with three tons of do-it-yourself dinosaur skeleton kits.

Now, if you look at a brontosaurus standing there munching on a tree with his head on one end and his tail on the other, he looks pretty symmetrical, and at least to me it's not immediately clear which end you're supposed to clip the head onto. Finally our exhibits guys, whose usual duties are to drill holes and paint things, checked some paleontology books out of the library and figured it out.

My own contributions were less intellectual. To vacuum-clean a newly-completed 8,000 square-foot dinosaur exhibit is to understand the very definition of housework. It's like cleaning an airport, only there's always an allosaurus tail ready to poke you in the ear. I guess that when dinosaurs walked the earth, each one held his long tail with the tip elevated to the precise height of the human face. Despite repeated cautions from the boss and my own concern over having to write 'poked by dinosaur tail' under Cause of Injury, I managed to vacuum myself backwards into the bony embrace of the tyrannosaurus, realistically posed in a lunchtime attack on the stegosaurus. Amid the coarse laughter of my fellow workers I found myself locked between the two great, skeletal thunder lizards, trying to extricate myself and the vacuum cleaner with someone's rib wrapped around my neck.

And so we opened the exhibit on schedule, though some of our Jurassic friends weren't standing quite upright, and there was wet paint here and there. But the faithful dinosaur came through: the crowds loved them, and our museum was saved to fight another day.

Buick Propelled by Lungs, Luck, and Prayer

It was July, 1992, a holiday weekend. We'd retrieved our friends Jeannie and Dean at the airport in Jackson, Mississippi and begun the 125-mile journey to our home in Starkville. Then the noble 1981 Buick Skylark stopped dead.

Now, Dean and I are both engineers and a bit jealous of our automobile-repair prowess. He's a better mechanic than I am, but I find weirder ways to fix things.

We dove under the hood. There was no gas in the carburetor, but the fuel filters were clean. This was not so great because it meant that the fuel pump was shot.

It was a warm night. We growled around under the hood, considering alternatives. The women finished rolling their eyes at us and settled down to serious reminiscing, and whatever else it is that women talk about—probably plotting the downfall of Men.

Dean and I concurred, at least when it came to the Men at GM's Buick Division. They had decided to mount the fuel pump in this particular V-6 next to the hot exhaust pipes. They then tried to make up for this keen arrangement by adding special pipes to cool the pump with extra gasoline circulated from the tank. This is the sort of cutting-edge innovation that made GM what it is today, i.e., in big trouble.

Dean considered more conventional solutions while I contemplated the scrap auto parts in the trunk. Among them was a big radiator hose (used) a length of one-inch heater hose (also used, and greasy) and a wire coat hanger.

Dean was convinced that we'd have to rig a hose and a bottle to drip gas into the carburetor as we drove. But I thought that maybe, if we could somehow apply pressure to the air space above the fuel in the tank, the gas would be forced up through the fuel line past the bad fuel pump to the carburetor.

I now know that God protects his feebler children, for the end of the big hose fit perfectly into the gas filler neck. I spliced the thin heater hose to the big radiator hose with some coat hanger wire. The strange assembly barely reached from the fuel filler pipe up through the back window, but it was enough.

I don't think Dean has ever had a generous assessment of my sanity, nor have the women. But I figured that if I sat in the rear seat with the window rolled down, I could apply enough pressure by mouth through the unspeakable black hose to maintain fuel pressure to the engine. It worked: Natalie turned the key, the car started, and we were off.

In two miles my eyes were bulging from their sockets. I learned to maintain pressure in the tank by clamping the hose shut with my teeth while I took the next breath through my nose. Gradually ascending the learning curve, we discovered that the car would run okay on the level, but that I had to wheeze vigorously to get us up the hills.

It is said that the Lord looks with favor upon the least of us, and this pretty much described Kinsler in the back seat of the Buick with his old buddy, the hose. It was the early hours of morning, the weather was good, the terrain fairly flat, and there weren't any Mississippi State Police around to inquire about our mobile fuel-inhaling parlor.

At 4:30 AM we glided into Starkville on a wing and a prayer. Visions of oil refineries danced in my vapor-laden head.

Dean and I replaced the fuel pump the next day. It lasted for six months.

Local Man Exhibits Brief Periods of Consciousness

I faint.

I have departed consciousness on a fairly regular basis since I was seven, when I was hanging from a railing in the gym at Coventry School and cracked my tailbone a good one. I'd endured worse, but this time I began to feel cold, and sweaty, and then—nothing. I was at peace. Well, at least I was at peace until a chorus of voices began screaming "Mark!!" into both ears. I opened my eyes to see a circle of faces above me, faces that showed a lot more concern than usual.

Since then I have developed an exquisitely honed set of reflexes which, when triggered by any of a distressingly long list of stimuli, cause Kinsler to sever all communications. It's so embarrassing that I'm glad I'm unconscious.

Needles will do it. There was an episode of *Mission: Impossible* where someone got a spinal injection and a cranial injection so the enemy would think he'd had a stroke, and I really wish I hadn't watched that particular part of it one night in the TV room at Ohio State. My friends told me that I had tried to leave but didn't quite make it: some unsuspecting colleagues arrived just then and when they opened the door I fell out onto them, eyes rolled back in my head. As I say, it's embarrassing.

Sudden pain will do it. Natalie has recovered my limp corpse several times: once from the bathtub when I had a kidney stone, once from the front lawn when I twisted my ankle, and twice from the couch when I strained my back.

Bad news will do it. One fine morning a graduate school secretary told me that I was in serious trouble for something. She was mistaken, but fifteen years later they still tell of how I dropped in my tracks.

Eye drops will do it. A very busy and important and overpriced New Haven eye doctor and his attractive, efficient assistant ignored my spluttered warnings. She briskly pried my eyelids open, and when I awoke on the carpeted floor of their elaborate office there were two overpriced physicians (from adjacent elaborate offices) yelling and trying to take my blood pressure at the same time. It turned out that (1) the eye doctor lived in mortal fear of lawsuits and thought he'd killed me, and (2) I had brought down the attractive, efficient assistant by collapsing on her.

Nowadays an eye doctor need only say 'howdy' to send the blood to my feet and my body slumping to the floor. My defense is that I have no control over the matter: if I find myself chanting that I will not, will *not* faint, it means that I'm on final approach to Blackout International.

Intravenous medical procedures will do it. The other day I passed out during one of those x-ray procedures where they inject dye to outline your entrails for the camera. It didn't help one bit that they made me listen to, read, and sign a delectably-long list of possible side effects from the dye injection that I was about to undergo, including warmth, nausea, and death.

I would really like to donate blood, honest. But I'm sorry: I tell the Red Cross that I've just gotten out of prison. For drug offenses. In Haiti. With my partner, Marcel. Who died. They probably don't need A-positive anyway.

And about all I can say about capital punishment by lethal injection is that they'll never take me alive. I'd just drop dead thinking about it, and nobody'd have to bother.

Poor Natalie. She is so patient, and I am so lucky.

And They Say It Still Roams the Interstate: Tales of the 1970 Volkswagen

My sister was proud of her first car, a shiny blue 1970 Volkswagen Beetle. But Miriam really drives an automobile, and by the time I inherited it seven hard years later the poor vehicle had profound problems in every vital system. Generations of field mice had built their lives and families in the main fuse box, the right front brakes were reduced to iron scrapings, ferocious Cleveland rust had consumed much of the thin VW frame, and there were antique French fries down in the seats.

But it ran, and Connecticut didn't have auto safety inspections then. I replaced the front brakes, patched the frame with sheet metal screws, and installed a temperature gauge because the little engine tended to overheat.

After three more years of semi-faithful service, the body gradually settled onto the axles from the rust. That was why the steering wheel shaft started to scrape and then broke off completely during a U-turn one fine evening, leaving me with a steering wheel that was no longer connected to anything. I fixed it with a couple of bolts and a piece of rubber hose.

I made sort of a science project out of keeping the engine cool. You have to: the air-cooled VW engine will seize in an instant if it overheats.

So I tried dripping water into the fan from a soda bottle mounted upside-down on the firewall, which actually works fairly well. I ran oil lines in from the engine so I'd have somewhere to hang the extra oil cooler. And then one day I read that a VW will run lots cooler if you block the air flow around the engine because then the fan won't pull in hot air.

If you ever do that, don't use wads of newspaper. The Young Engineer was riding the Pennsylvania Turnpike on a visit to Pittsburgh when the smoke rose and the engine died. I pulled off the road and frantically switched off the ignition key. Having thus locked the steering wheel, I mowed down Milepost 278 like a stalk of grain at the harvest, but at least I stopped.

The engine was on fire! The tarred paper heater hoses were aflame! Pull them out! Smear right hand with burning tar!

A trucker with a fire extinguisher rescued me, and I set to work with my injured paw to try to fix the car before the state police found me. At least I managed to bend Milepost 278 reasonably erect by the time the cruiser pulled up.

The Pennsylvania Turnpike has a free ambulance, and they made me ride in it to the hospital. The nurse cleaned off the tar with mineral oil and bandaged me up. I have patient, loyal friends who have learned to expect almost anything, and this time it was Susan who retrieved me.

The next day I bought new ignition parts to replace the burned ones. Then back out to Milepost 278, where poor Susan installed the new parts under my instruction because I only had the use of one hand.

The car started and we drove back. Since the VW ran fine with its new ignition system, I drove it for another six months until winter, when I finally bought a truck.

Still, I wouldn't give up. I towed the relic back to Connecticut and sold it to a guy who paid me eighty bucks for it since it ran. Then he examined the vehicle more closely and nearly wept. I offered to give him back his money, but he just shook his head and waved me away.

I still have the truck.

The Engineer in the Garden

Our garden is at peace now. The combat is over; the final trumpet has sounded. All that remains is to render a final spading and to gather in this year's plant stakes.

I am obsessed by garden stakes. Every year there's a new plan.

The plant support scheme two years ago used arches to support the plants. Because it's the cheapest form of pipe, I built my support arches from floppy gray plastic electrical conduit, the tubes that electricians mount in houses and run wires through. It was a great idea: just pound two holes in the ground about five feet apart, bend the tubing into a semi-circle and insert the ends into the holes to make a big arch. Then, simply tie strings along the arch at twelve-inch intervals and let them dangle down to the young peas or beans or tomatoes. The plants will grab the strings and pull themselves up. The arches are unobtrusive, they won't rust or rot, and they'll pop right out of the ground when we're done in the fall. Why bother with a stake for each plant?

Well, I found out why: when the plants grab the string to pull themselves up, they pull the arch down. In a couple of weeks the arches were all flopped sideways, the plants and strings in a hopeless tangle on the ground.

Okay, we'll brace them. My structural engineering books say that two intersecting arches form a stable structure, not unlike a dome. Pound more holes, add another arch perpendicular to and just beneath the original, and tie them where they intersect with a plastic tie strap. Looks like an X from above.

Dangle new strings down, have wife perform a surgical separation of the plants tangled up from the previous attempt, tie new strings to the plants.

And then wait for another week for the plants to collapse the arches, or domes, right down to the carefully-tilled earth. They still looked like X's from above, but they were X's that were flat on the ground.

That was two years ago, and I'm still trying to find uses for 20 ten-foot pieces of permanently-curved half-inch plastic electrical conduit. I eliminated part of the storage problem when I forgot I'd laid them on the ground, the grass grew over them and I hit them with the lawnmower and thus manufactured some swell gray plastic mulch.

Last year was the plastic netting. It would be great: I'd just discovered that you can buy plastic versions of almost any kind of wire fencing. Okay: if we stretch some 2" x 2" plastic fence along the rows, the plants will grab onto the fence and pull themselves up. I was cautious this time: I used good solid stakes to support the fencing.

But when they finally get going, our plants are awfully vigorous. It was but the work of a moment, which in Garden Time equals ten business days, for Nature to collapse the works of Man into yet another tangled mess. The Peoples' Harvest Brigade griped that she couldn't pick anything because our garden was now a gulag of vegetables imprisoned beneath tangles of plastic fence.

I got smart this year. No fooling around: I made real stakes out of steel pipe. One stake per plant. It was a sea of stakes. Every plant tied up carefully. It worked fine until the drought, and then the invasion of volunteer cherry tomatoes and then the morning glories.

Once again, Kinsler tasted defeat. But we love cherry tomatoes, and the morning glories were magnificent. I'll start spading after the next frost.

M Kinsler Absorbs the Wisdom of the Ages

Education specialists tell us that children gain much of their knowledge from their peers. Here is a partial compilation of what I was told by age 9:

(1) You have to eat a pound of dirt before you die.

(2) People die because they run out of air. So every time you breathe, someone dies somewhere because you've used up their air.

(3) If you didn't go to school, you wouldn't know how to talk, or anything.

(4) The police will come and arrest you if you take that tag off the mattress.

(5) You can kill someone by hitting them in the nose real hard so that their nose-bone pushes up into their brain.

(6) Some guy tried to survive being in the electric chair by putting a series of nails underneath his skin from his head all the way down to his foot.

(7) If you poke at the bottom of a pond with a stick and bubbles come up, it's quicksand.

(8) Those berries are poisonous.

(9) If you run on a concrete sidewalk, you'll fall and your head will break open.

(10) New York is in Ohio.

(11) Robots from Venus might really attack Earth sometime.

(12) If everyone in China jumped off a chair at the same time, they could cause an earthquake in the United States.

(13) There was a guy who killed four kids. He said that he wanted to reduce the excess school population.

(14) If you dropped a penny from the Empire State Building, it would kill somebody.

(15) If you fell out of an airplane, you'd die of fright before you hit the ground.

(16) If you're real, real, real smart, you'll go crazy someday.

(17) There was a woman who was driving along and hit these pipes that were hanging off the back of a truck. The pipes cut off her head, and they found it in the trunk.

(18) Your third-grade school record will stay with you for the rest of your life.

(19) Teachers all live at the school.

(20) Your blood is just sort of poured around inside you.

(21) A lady got so scared that all her hair turned white.

(22) If you swallow an acorn just before you die an oak tree will grow out of your body and up out of your grave.

(23) Those berries are poisonous.

(24) It feels different to be a girl than it does to be a boy.

(25) Everybody sees colors differently. Your green is different from my green.

(26) If you get blown up by a hand grenade, you'd just disappear.

(27) If you could dig all the way through the earth, you'd float around when you got to the middle.

(28) You could be outside playing or just walking around and suddenly you could drop dead right there.

(29) Buffalo Bob once got real mad at kids that weren't behaving on the Howdy Doody show and yelled at them.

(30) One of the legs of a mailbox is hollow, and the mail goes through it down into a tunnel underground.

(31) It's against the law to commit suicide. If you do it and it doesn't work, they'll arrest you and put you in jail.

We gratefully acknowledge the following contributors: my sister (2, 4, 8, 11, 24, 29), my friend Robby (3, 7), fellow scholars in the Cleveland Heights Public Schools (5, 6, 10, 13-18, 19-27, 31), me (22, 30), and the Barenholtz sisters (1, 9, 28), who lived next door and tried to stuff dirt into my mouth. And I read (12) in Newsweek when I was in my 30's.

You'll have to sketch an illustration here* because I can't draw.

***unless this is a library book.**

All I Need Is a Tall Ship, and a Star to Steer Her By

The proper procedure in running away to sea is to slip away from the family farm early one morning and head over the English countryside to Hull or Portsmouth, where the captain reckons ye a likely lad and you put your mark on the papers. You do not run away to sea by taking the bus downtown after your mother sees the ad in the Cleveland Plain Dealer one morning and tells you to go, which is what I did.

By 1966 the cruise ship *South American*, owned by Georgian Bay Lines and built along the graceful lines of a World War I destroyer, had plowed the Great Lakes from Montreal to Duluth for fifty years. The Line's latest marketing effort was to hire college kids as waitresses and kitchen workers. In their off-hours the kids would entertain the passengers (bring your guitar, suggested the brochure) thus lending youth and liveliness to an old ship filled with old passengers.

They sent me to the Coast Guard office to get my Merchant Marine Certificate, a plastic card emblazoned with anchors. The photograph shows the usual stunned-looking young M Kinsler gazing out at his future through thick-rimmed glasses.

Then I walked up the gangplank and into glory, shouldering a sea bag formerly used by my sister for laundry. Accommodations were below the water line, where a quarter-inch of vintage steel separated me from the world's largest inland body of fresh water. The steel bunks were bolted to the wall, and when the engine was running it was like sleeping in a washing machine.

My daily commute wound through three-foot-wide steel passageways and up ladders, ending when I popped my head through a hatchway into the pantry, where I helped make salads and ladle food from the steam table to waitresses passing through with the plates.

The cooks liked me. They'd been Pullman porters; legendary attendants on luxury express trains who served meals for dozens of dining car passengers from kitchens smaller than ours. They smiled at my enthusiasm—a rare commodity among the youthful workers that year—and discovered that I could be sent on errands and return promptly with the requested item.

The trays of entrees and vats of soup came up a little elevator from the kitchen below and manhandled to the steam tables. We lavished three sumptuous meals per day on our seven hundred passengers from a combined facility smaller than the kitchen of a Domino's Pizza.

I spent hours watching the ancient brass-and-steel quadruple-expansion steam engine, last of its kind and tall as a two-story house, flail its seven-foot piston rods to drive us along at 25 mph. We sailed west to Minnesota, and east through the Thousand Islands to Quebec. We put in at Ogdensburg, New York for their bagpipe festival, and at Montreal, where I got lost. The Lakes get rough toward fall, and the ship rolled a good ten degrees: if you timed things right, you always walked downhill.

Convivial as ever, I never learned to make friends in that odd social environment, but I was fascinated with the ships, the lakes, and the old lake sailors. When the autumn school term approached they let me off at the dock in Cleveland and I took the bus home.

I never saw the ship again. She failed a safety inspection and the Coast Guard ordered her off the lakes and they towed her away. Plans to use her as a merchant marine academy fell through, and she lay abandoned near Baltimore until they broke her up in 1992.

They say a sailor never forgets his first ship, and I grieve for her.

Spring: When Old Guys, Old Projects and Rusted Bolts Find Renewal

After months of dreaming and strategizing, my fantasies are becoming reality, for on this Sunday afternoon of warm temperatures, cool grass, and soft breezes I have at last resumed the restoration of my old truck. Today's exercise addresses the engine, specifically a loud and leaky cast-iron exhaust manifold which must be removed and then properly re-sealed to the cylinder head.

It is not a vehicle that we use much. A winter repair job on one of the real cars requires nights spent on the garage floor, fighting it out with metric fasteners under shop lights and a feeble electric heater. But the repair of a non-essential, beloved old truck is like baseball, performed in peace and dignity when the grass is green and the sun shines.

Through nights of sleet and days of chill rain, I have lulled myself to sleep by planning, in exquisite detail, how I will fix the manifold. I'll have to pull the starter to reach the rear bolts, and perhaps I can pivot the alternator down to clear the front ones. I close my eyes to once again visualize how the engine compartment is laid out, and suddenly it's next morning, with ice pellets beating against the awnings of our little house. There is other work to be done, and the truck will remain entombed beneath ice out in the yard.

The season passes, but those first days of spring weather are neither peaceful nor dignified. The long, treacherous winter has rendered us distrustful of decent weather, and lest we miss an ice-free day we descend into a flurry of long-deferred activity. The retreat of the East Mulberry Street Glacier from our front yard uncovers layers of winter neglect.

Then there's the garden, its soil to be strategized, pulverized and fertilized. The soil analysis says we're short on nitrogen, potassium, sulfur and probably osmium. I hurriedly spade in little bags of soil supplements. Hurry: it can't last; it'll start raining forever again. Natalie's weather-obsessed friend Cathe gleefully predicts snow by the end of the week. Woe unto us, for the peas should have been planted and the grapevines pruned already.

That, and Natalie loves the spring daffodils. Lest they freeze over tomorrow, we take long walks and drives to maximize her exposure to our daffodils and everyone else's daffodils.

But now it's April, and the promise of spring has been kept. The weather has held for a week, the daffodils have apparently proved sufficient, and our mansion's garden and grounds are somewhat better.

And so on this mild Sunday afternoon she has tripped off to Columbus to shop, leaving me with the last of the spring responsibilities, and I finish the grapevines and peas, and then on my way through the garage I find my disorderly box of socket wrenches. Just outside the door, parked in the soft, sunlit grass is my truck, and it is waiting for me.

The generator doesn't have to come all the way out, and the tough bolt on the starter wasn't so bad. The ten manifold bolts are the true challenge, but I can declare a small victory as each comes free, and lie for a moment as the blossom-scented breeze blows past me, there beneath the engine. As I quit for the day, two bolts are still holding out, but the summer lies ahead.

I lie down for a short nap. I'll use new stainless steel bolts, and high-temperature Permatex. But gasket compounds require faith, hope and sometimes prayer to work. Maybe I'll just use a new gasket and seal it right this time. Or, I could put on stainless steel studs, and then nuts….zzzzzz.

The Devil Lives in That Bottle

"You guzzle that stuff," said She.

"I do not 'guzzle' it," I replied.

But as always, she was right. Demon Big K Cola is a larger part of my life than it probably should be, and my beverage habits match some of those seven danger signs I've read about. For example, "Has this habit ever caused arguments with spouse or family?"

Well, yes. There was the time that I decided to keep one of those twelve-packs of cans upright in the refrigerator, like you're supposed to, extracting one can at a time out of the little slot, and it would have been great if the side of the thing hadn't torn, dropping six cans of Big K on the floor and rupturing three of them. One was particularly ambitious, spraying sticky fizzy brown fluid out of a hole in its side as it rolled to the other side of the kitchen, casting elegant spirals of the stuff on floor and walls with each revolution.

"Has this habit altered your personal life?" Well, no, really.

Well, yes, really, for I mostly buy Big K in two-liter bottles, and to someone whose creativity exceeds his organizational skills an unbreakable, transparent container is irresistible, especially if it's free.

There are so many uses. A bottle, label removed and slit up one side, makes a perfect small parts container if you hang it from a hook, only here we encounter an artistic controversy: I do not consider these 'hideous,' nor do I feel they should be relegated to the garage, which is where they are now.

I have discovered that one of those bicycle pumps that looks like a piece of a broomstick will just fit down the neck of an empty bottle. Vigorous pumping raises the internal pressure such that when released, the bottle becomes an impromptu rocket that bounces vigorously off ceiling and walls just prior to the researcher being sent outside with it. Additional research revealed that if you fill it halfway up with water first, it will reach an altitude of some 100 feet while drenching your upturned face.

Raw material storage is always a challenge for the bottle addict. The empties, washed and carefully placed on the floor near the back door for later disposition, can be accidentally kicked across the floor, yielding great clangor and expressions of exasperation not normally uttered by my beloved. My solution was to store them in the basement, which worked until it started to fill up down there. (The gas meter reader diplomatically withheld comment.) For a while I would simply throw empties in the general direction of the basement hatchway and listen to them bump and bang their way harmlessly down the stairs. The cat, however, failed to see the amusement value in this when, as he padded up the stairs upon a tour of exploration, a mistimed two-liter bottle came bouncing down at him.

Like most women, Natalie is reluctant to reveal her true feelings, but I sense that her patience with my Save The Earth With Soda Bottles movement could be wearing thin. But she doomed herself when she inadvertently expressed admiration for my idea of storing Christmas garland in them (you just feed the stuff into the neck, leaving a bit sticking out) and for my automatic ivy-growing bottles that gather rainwater in a funnel to supply the roots of the ivy sprig beneath.

As things stand, she is thankful that I have decided not to pursue my plan to build a lightweight air compressor tank by connecting dozens of the bottles together. And I am thankful that she is.

OSU Tri-Athlete Relates Early Hardships

I do not know if Ohio State University still requires it, but in 1965 you had to take three quarters of physical education. Yep: more gym, after I'd barely escaped with my life from the athletic dungeons of Cleveland Heights High School. My roommate, T. Craig Hawkins, observed that it was only one day per week, and there were some choices, and that it was better than going to Viet Nam.

The first term wasn't too bad: it was a golden autumn, and there was soccer, a sport that I more or less understood. I even scored a goal, once, though I believe that it may have been disallowed because my methodology involved running while I was looking sideways, thus tripping over the goalie and waking up entangled in the yellow netting of the goal structure.

For winter quarter, I signed up for boxing. I don't know: it just seemed sort of antique, the last of the old-fashioned courses of the 1800's, and I can't imagine that they offer it anymore. The instructor was a compact guy in his thirties, probably a public school teacher working on a master's degree and sentenced to teach our bunch as a condition of graduation. The first three weeks of the vague ten-week curriculum consisted of our sitting there on the floor in our Ohio State gym uniforms to hear the evils of professional boxing as currently practiced. I concurred that pro boxing was indeed corrupt and brutal, though I don't remember ever seriously considering it as an alternative to electrical engineering.

We finally got down to business and learned the rules of the Marquis of Queensberry, and what a right cross and a left hook were. As snow fell outside the huge gymnasium windows, we paired off to practice on each other. The guy I drew was sort of a closet intellectual like me and we silently agreed not to hurt each other. This worked for a couple of weeks, though T. Craig suggested that if we'd been Roman gladiators our sole entertainment value would have been as lion feed.

It was all pretty strange, standing there kind of poking at each other. Then one day my sparring partner didn't show up, and I found myself toe-to-toe with a short, sturdy guy who probably majored in Revenge Science and was clearly frustrated with our weeks of inaction. And so Kinsler learned the manly art of bobbing, weaving, and begging.

In the spring I registered for the freshman lacrosse team, which was really just another phys ed course. I thought it was cool because in 1965 nobody outside the Province of Quebec knew what lacrosse was. I bought a lacrosse stick, which looks like a combination hockey stick and snow shoe and ran around with it, trying to stay upright on the slippery grass. One day we ran through a spring football practice to be pursued by and yelled at by a loud gentleman later identified as Woody Hayes.

And then the year was over, and with it my lifetime athletic career. But I'd showed up faithfully each day, and occasionally the coach felt obliged to congratulate Kinsler, the class alien, for really trying out there.

I don't know. To this day I don't quite understand team sports. I think I'm as competitive as the next guy, but when I go out there and do what the coach says I'm supposed to do, everything feels like it's translated from the ancient Urdu epics.

But though I've never bridged the gap between my universe and that of my athlete friends, we've learned to exist together in peace. Perhaps there's some teamwork in that, after all.

Apparently the Almighty wants me to have soup in a cup.

Everybody knows that a calm, confident, competent person has strong, steady hands. Shakiness means that you're nervous, maybe because you feel guilty about something, or that you're seriously ill.

Though my competence is debatable even among friends, I am not sick and I don't feel very guilty about anything. But my hands shake, and they shake a lot.

It's called "essential tremor" disorder, and even a mild case is embarrassing. There's no real cure; apparently one of my genes dropped a valve back in 1947.

When I was eight the doctor had me hold a sheet of paper on my outstretched fingertips. It shook, so he prescribed tranquilizers, which didn't work. But I've always been able to compensate: I learned to repair watches and electronics, and things were okay.

Not any longer. It has gotten to the point where I have a tough time with simple stuff. I can do just about anything I need to, but only after multiple attempts and some planning. When I work on the car it's a foregone conclusion that I will drop a screw or two into the grass or down between the exhaust manifold and the Outer Hebrides.

But I am vastly better off than many people with this odd malady. I met a businessman and a university administrator who can't work because their tremors became so severe. A fine lady I worked with can no longer teach; her head shook, her voice quavered, and she often could not type. She spotted my slight tremor long before I noticed hers; it's a skill you acquire.

For me, it's just inconvenient. Eating has become strange, and my handwriting was rotten anyway. When I give science demonstrations for little kids I bumble around with my beakers and wires, looking like Old Dr Science, just out of rehab on work-release.

The kids ask, "Why do your hands shake?" It's fun to watch their parents try to sink into the floor with embarrassment, but there's an easy answer. I ask them to hold up one hand. Your hand stays steady, I tell them, because the muscles in the front of your hand are pulling against the muscles in the back of your hand. In my hands, I explain, the muscles are very polite, so they take turns pulling. The kids laugh. "Okay," they say.

Sometimes muscles I didn't know I had will vibrate with an invigorating buzz, down in my giblets. When I first set my cell phone to vibrate silently rather than ringing, I'd occasionally answer it and find that my spleen was calling in to say howdy.

The tremor support group meets in Hilliard once a month. I've learned there that people with tremors are typically more intelligent than average, and that you can reduce a hand tremor with a shot of whiskey. Beyond that, there are various medicines offered by neurologists, and you cope.

Most of the tremor literature is about Parkinson's disease, which kills you, so I am grateful to be alive and quivering. But I worry about people with ET who are ashamed of it, who fear for their jobs if the boss sees them shaking. It's tough to hide: I'll fumble a pen or splash coffee onto someone, and then I have to present the neurology lecture.

I don't know if my condition will get any worse. ET is supposed to be progressive, but I'm already so old that it probably won't get much farther before I stop moving altogether. Natalie says that she will take care of me in the meantime.

The East Mulberry Street Wind Power Project

With the purchase and installation of a final switch plate, I have today completed the installation of our seventh ceiling fan. With three upstairs and four downstairs, we just have to turn them all on at once and then we can begin air-commuter service to Gahanna.

The original light fixtures in this place were cool futuristic old glass things, and I thought they were great. But there is a short person whose idea of coolth does not encompass home décor purchased from the clearance rack at Hickle's Department Store in 1941, and she has mandated their replacement by fans equipped with attractive light sets, phooey.

Lowe's gets a hundred and fourteen bucks to install a ceiling fan, and I can certify here that they earn it. By the time I'd finished the first one (in her bedroom, of course) I felt like I'd just completed a scale model of the *Flying Cloud.*

I've gotten better at it over the years. The first step in the established ritual is to buy the fan and place it, still in its box, in the middle of the floor of the Targeted Room. This symbolizes that I have promised to install it, and marks the beginning of the Seasoning Period, in which the fan sits there until the box becomes a familiar and recognized part of the room décor, typically serving as a little coffee table after a while.

She recognized this ploy of old, so eventually I have to get to work already. Natalie always wants me to turn off all the power in the house whenever I do anything electrical, and if I don't she'll stand there with a broom, waiting to pry my quivering body from the wiring when the need arises.

Then it's time to read the installation instructions. They're printed with great cleverness: if you read the book from the front, the directions are in French. But if you turn it over and read from the back, they're in Spanish. I prefer the latter, where men are *hombres*, fans are *ventiladors*, and screws are *tornillos,* to be tightened *firmemente*.

Most of the paperwork is legal warnings, wherein the *hombre* learns that if he tries to install a thirty-pound fan in a structure with a Styrofoam ceiling, or perhaps in a tent, it will twist loose and commence chopping its way through the neighborhood, teetering along on its frosted-glass light set and menacing small children with its brass-mounted Frosted Beech paddles as it heads toward the Interstate.

But you couldn't tear our ancient steel junction boxes out with a fork lift, so I just mount the brackets and wire the wiring, eventually getting to the point where we find that the holes for the numerous *tornillos* in the fan housing don't always line up so swell, especially when you're trying to squeeze the little remote-control receiver up inside the cover plate on the ceiling.

Deep inside this receiver lurks a tiny code switch, carefully set at the factory to respond to telemetric commands from some kid playing with a radio-controlled Hot Wheels Barbie two blocks away. After days spent trying to determine just how the cats were contriving to turn the new fan on each afternoon, I had to get back up there, pull everything apart, and re-set the switch to a code that I dearly hope does not correspond to the one on our neighbor's garage door opener.

But it is done, and now that I've gotten good at the task there will be no more to install.

"It really looks nice," she said.

Welcome, Race Fans

It had been a rough winter, and Natalie wanted to find spring. Spring, and especially daffodils. Normally the most domestic of creatures, she was restless, ranging about the house as her spring break ticked away. I found the road atlas and began calculating. We had three days.

"Well," I said, fussing with the ruler and the scale of miles. "We can try for Lookout Mountain. There was a song that said we should see Rock City." She is not a devotee of country music, but was satisfied when shown that Rock City was very far south of snow-covered East Mulberry Street.

We held the customary pre-trip ceremony, solemnly looking at each other and agreeing that neither of us wished to go anywhere, and then we got moving, following I-71 south through snow, rain, sleet, and Cincinnati. We crossed into Kentucky, where I spotted her first patch of roadside daffodils and a forsythia bush in reluctant bloom. We outran the weather and pounded south to Chattanooga, right up to the top of Lookout Mountain and into Rock City, which was closed.

Natalie demanded the true South, and was happy only after we finally dropped to earth in Dalton, Georgia. The trees were in bloom, there were daffodils, and a nutty mockingbird sat outside singing to us the entire night.

We tried going east to find more spring before turning north towards home. But this placed us on the wrong side of the Great Smoky Mountains, and nobody has yet built an Interstate highway across them to Lancaster.

So I plotted out a picturesque route. We would go to Kingsport Tennessee, find a motel early in the evening for a change, and in the morning we'd wind north on US Route 23, up through the mountains of Kentucky and West Virginia to the Ohio River.

Now, we have always considered ourselves an observant pair, intelligent and keenly cognizant of our surroundings. Well, we aren't: at the motel in Kingsport we didn't notice the oddly-decorated cars that crowded its driveway, nor that its lounge was jammed with festive young men. The desk clerks looked at us when we asked for a room, beholding with dazzled eyes the only couple in the hemisphere who didn't know that the NASCAR season was opening that day in nearby Bristol. All those "Welcome Race Fans" signs began to make sense: every room from the Shenandoah to the Euphrates had been booked for months.

We got into the car and drove north, hoping to outrun NASCAR. East Tennessee coal country is not like Ohio's: the mountains are high, gray stone walls, and they block the sun from the tiny towns below. Suddenly things didn't look so friendly, spring notwithstanding, and it was getting dark.

Somewhere past Gate City we found a strip center with a motel that wouldn't rate a single star even in the highly-flexible Kinsler Motor Club listings, but we were getting tired. Did they have a room? Sure, said the clerk. One hundred forty dollars. We looked at each other and simultaneously recited, "Welcome, race fans."

He lowered the price to a hundred as we reached the door but we kept going, finally dropping off NASCAR radar at a motel in Pikeville. The brochure in the room celebrated the region's fame: it is the historic center of the Hatfield-McCoy feud.

But the weather was kind, and next morning Spring followed us right up US23 into Ohio. We turned off at Chillicothe and followed country roads through old Victorian towns toward home. We watched the yards for E-G newspaper tubes, and the first one we saw had daffodils blooming around it.

Local Couple Celebrates the Change in Seasons

It began when I crawled into bed last night and strayed from the paths of righteousness. For there beneath the covers, left unprotected by the owner, lay a defenseless leg, perfectly situated for the warming of a chilled foot. The shriek rocketed the sleeping cat to parts unknown, and the bill of particulars was read: "I just got warmed up," she griped.

Well, she hadn't. I felt her nose, and it was cold, indicating that by extension, the entire female attached thereto was cold as well. Okay, I said. Let's get out the electric blanket.

No, no, no. Maybe just one of the little blankets from the guest room, no more, said she.

We tried that last night, and that's why we didn't sleep. It's cold.

We go through this every year. I got up, dug out the Sunbeam and its tangle of controls from the Blanket Library in the guest room and, ignoring muffled protests from the chilled person beneath pulled off the thin summer quilt, spread the blanket over her, and laid the quilt over that.

In my time I have wired electric guitars and part of a radio station, but little can compare to installing the wiring harness of a dual-control electric blanket at two in the morning. I untangled the wires, stretched them out on the bedroom floor in a rough outline of the final configuration, and then set to work, spelunking deep into cat territory to connect the power plug, clipping the controls to the headboard, routing the inter-control wiring, and finally running the three-conductor feed line to the foot of the bed, where I found that the plug did not fit the socket in the blanket.

Jamming them together did not help. Neither did staring at them intently in the hope that the pins in the plug would somehow prove to be extremely flexible. I looked on the blanket shelf: perhaps there was some sort of plug adapter that I'd forgotten about. At least she was more relaxed: the unpowered blanket itself was keeping her warmer.

I sat and thought, and dim memories returned. We'd bought a new blanket last winter, and found that it was equipped with strange electronic controls. But the controls I had just installed were simple and non-electronic. Conclusion: they were the wrong controls, and I knew where the right ones were.

The old blanket was in the guest-room closet, packed up for a trip to Goodwill Industries along with the set of controls for the new one. I dug them out and wearily set about the work of dismantling the earlier installation, diving once again under the bed to reach the power plug.

The only bright spot in re-doing most jobs is that it's generally faster the second time, and the new plug fit the socket on the blanket. But now the lights on the controls were flashing to signal that something was wrong. I unplugged the control line from the blanket, turned each control off and on, and adjusted the temperature settings. Nothing.

Okay, Kinsler: think. There must be a microprocessor, and it is somehow stuck in a software loop. Reset it.

I crawled down into Box Spring Caverns once again, unplugged the power plug, waited ten seconds for the power-supply capacitors to discharge, and plugged it back in. The flashing stopped and the blanket began to warm up. She turned over.

Muttering about technological milestones like electronic bedding that issues error codes, I stuffed the old controls into the bag with the old blanket and climbed in next to her, and we slept.

A brief appearance by a small visitor leaves a cat-shaped hole in our lives.

Natalie says that a cat will tell you his name if you listen carefully. The first one she gave him was Mister Grayhead, for he was sort of gray beneath his general dishevelment. His round face showed little expression, but the yellow-orange eyes were intense, silently asking for mercy and understanding. He would roll on the ground when he saw Natalie.

He'd been hanging out for most of the winter at our outdoor food bowl, and alone among its clients seemed to want to come into the house; we'd see him propped up on his front paws, looking through the lower glass of our storm door into our distinctly uninviting 'mud room.' But he was all cat, and all male, a combat veteran covered with battle scars won in cat wars over the temptresses of East Mulberry Street.

Natalie loved him. We currently have two cats in residence, but we're FAA-rated for three; we never replaced our dignified Marmalade after she left us a year ago. "Okay," she ordered, finally. "Get the cat carrier and we'll bring him in."

"We'll bring him in," I mused. Run, cat, I thought. Run fast, run far.

But I got out the carrier and a plastic bin to put it in, extra protection for Natalie's back seat in the event that cat protests in liquid form were issued on the way to the Operation. Natalie called the veterinarian's office to find out when their hours were: until seven p.m. weekdays, and eleven a.m. on Saturday. Then we waited.

Mr Grayhead must have called them too, for thereafter we never saw him except on Sundays, or after seven p.m. on weekdays. Last Saturday he showed up at the dish at eleven a.m. sharp.

But yesterday I went out to fret over the garden and behold, there he was, having lunch. Natalie was home to help, the vet was open and the stars had aligned. We closed intermediate doors, opened the outside door to the deck, and he strolled in, firm in step and looking around with the curious caution customary to cats. He didn't flick a whisker when the door slammed behind him, but just looked at us with those trusting eyes and said not a word all the way to the vet's office.

Okay, said the vet, all business. We'll clean him up, check him for cat diseases, and neuter him (ow ow ow ow, I volunteered, to nobody's amusement.) But when she cradled him in one arm to carry him to off a semi-private suite, he turned his mild face to gaze at her with those eyes, and she melted. Every vet likes every animal, but the look they exchanged in the little exam room was special. He was that sort of cat.

We came home. "I've betrayed you both," announced Natalie to the incumbents. They looked up at her without enthusiasm. "You're getting a new companion."

The telephone rang this morning. It was the vet, calling with very bad news: our gray cat had tested positive for feline immuno-deficiency virus. FIV is essentially cat AIDS, distantly related to the human disease, communicable and devastating if it is the active variety. If we kept him we would expose our pair to the disease, and letting him run loose would most likely sentence him to a lonely, excruciating death. My Columbus friend Becky, a cat-loving biologist, confirmed the death sentence.

Natalie has gone off to church this evening. He has told her that his real name was Sir Cedric Gray, and now there is one more candle to light.

Free Table

The dining room table my parents bought for our new house in Cleveland Heights in 1956 is round, fifty-two inches across, and surfaced with a soft black linoleum that I've never seen on anything claiming to be a practical piece of furniture. It picks up imprints of placemats, and ball-point pen. There are 8th-grade homework assignments from 1961 encoded somewhere on that tabletop.

It is, in short, one of those retro pieces of furniture that no home could be without in the 1950's, especially if you had ambitions like my parents and their ultra-fashionable interior decorator Isabel Lichtenstein. Isabel and her husband Roy, who went on to become a famous artist, apparently considered our family something of a challenge, but since I was nine I knew nothing about them.

What I do know is that this thing was sitting in a U-Haul storage locker and that it hadn't sold during its first outing on eBay. So for the next attempt I wrote a long, poetic description of our old, ultra-modern table, including several mentions of Roy Lichtenstein, like he'd painted it or something. I also said that I'd handle crating and shipping, which I shouldn't have.

It sold for two hundred bucks to a fellow in Florida. The celebration was brief, for now I had to build a crate. I can work with metal, sort of, but my efforts in wood always end up shaped like modern art. Still, there wasn't any alternative, so I got my beloved 1964 Econoline van running, retrieved the table, stopped at Lowe's for a sheet of heavy waferboard and assorted lumber, and roared home just as the truck's notorious carburetor began to flood.

It was like building a boat. Consider, if you will, a four-by-eight sheet of paneling and figure out how to use it to crate a table whose diameter is four and one-half feet, a table whose top is so delicate that salt shakers left imprints in it fifty years ago.

So I sawed off three feet of the waferboard and tacked and glued it to the five feet that were left, with an extra rib for reinforcement. Then came a ring of pieces sawed from a two-by-six to surround the sacred item once it was face-down on the heavy, protective paneling. The cover was a piece of Masonite, reshaped with pop rivets.

The result was a five-foot diameter wooden flying saucer weighing perhaps 150 pounds, and the shipping lady cheerfully told me that it would cost $535.00 for them to pick it up at our house. An outfit called freightquote.com, rescued me with a $125.00 shipping deal provided I could get the beast to a loading dock in Columbus.

I'm sure that I'll eventually sort out the memories, now repressed, containing the details of that trip. I know I made a platform from concrete blocks to get the saucer into the truck, and that there was a long, long ramp from my truck to the top of their loading dock, and that I had to take the carburetor apart twice.

The 1964 Econoline is an old design in which the engine is right next to the driver, and we sputtered home with the engine lid open and my hand cupped over the air intake, all the way back down US 33. Then I forgot that they were working on the streets here, and tried to take a shortcut down the narrow brick alleyways to get home, and there were cars coming the other way, and there might have been dragons, and herds of elk.

I sure hope they like our table in Florida.

The Hearty Pioneers Didn't Need Bathtub Caulk

Our upstairs bathroom is five feet wide, nine feet long and a hundred years old. The most recent historic restorations have left it with golden oak veneer cabinets (circa 1972), shrunken vinyl floor tiles, and a decaying tub enclosure of faux-tile Masonite. The bathtub is weary and pitted, and they never did get the shower quite right.

There was no shower rod, and nowhere to install one unless you wanted to screw one end into a window pane.

The Boy Scientist's leisurely consideration of possible engineering solutions sped right up when a short, plumbing-deprived person issued orders to get on with it already or she'd be hanging her shower curtain from his nose. The compromise, hastily constructed from a scrap of aluminum pipe and four sheetrock screws, remains in service.

The little knob thing on the bathtub faucet spout diverted maybe twenty percent of the water flow up to the shower head, leaving the rest to splash upon your feet while you took a shower. The shower head itself was somehow positioned such that a substantial portion of that twenty percent found its way along the rim of the tub and onto the floor unless you remembered to arrange a cleverly-folded bath towel to soak it up. And three applications of anti-mildew caulk around the bathtub only whetted the appetite of the immortal fungi that have lived there since the earth cooled.

So now the shower head resides at the end of a stylish extension made of half-inch galvanized steel pipe and, where the faucet spout used to be, a stub of pipe capped with a big white PVC ball valve emerges from the wall. The shower turns on when you twist the sporty red handle.

The bathroom cabinet I built was supposed to look rustic. I have since learned that it's a bad idea for me to start any project with the intention of making it look rustic. It would have looked rustic enough if I'd aimed for French Provincial. What we got looks like it's made out of planks pried from a shipwreck.

And so we are going to throw in the towel, so to speak, and have someone besides me come in and renovate our bathroom. Replace the tub, replace the tub surround, replace the vanity, and tile the place. (We won't bother with the four-person-far-infrared sauna, the wine rack, the computerized steam shower, or the fireplace.)

But bathroom renovations can take some time, so before we begin we will have to figure out alternate bathing arrangements. We discussed the installation of a shower in the half-bath downstairs, but according to our Lancaster Police Department yardstick the only way to install a real shower stall in there would be to take out the toilet. We'll have to devise something smaller unless we plan to hang a bucket with holes punched in the bottom from a pole in the back yard.

So the other night we bought one of those hand shower things that looks like a telephone receiver, and I found a large galvanized washtub in which I shall cut a drain hole. The hose will run into the basement, I will hang a shower curtain around the washtub, somehow, and we'll be all ready for holiday entertaining.

It might work, but I must admit that I am not altogether comfortable asking my beloved, a scholar respected in her field and author of papers in academic journals, to shower in a washtub. But she has a sense of humor and, closely related, a tolerance for one M Kinsler that seems unlimited.

A Christmas Story

Our garden this year yielded yet another bountiful crop of succulent, ready-to-eat morning glories, and we were waiting for the first frost to kill them off when we saw him, a black shape silent in the tangle of vines. All black cats bear a strong family resemblance—they look as though someone has carved a cat-shaped piece out of the world, perhaps to catch mice in another dimension—but this one wasn't ours. He has green eyes, for one thing, and he's slimmer and more graceful than our 12-year-old Mr. Shadow, veteran of many helpings of Mature Blend cat food.

The garden cat has been hanging around ever since, spending the daylight hours curled serenely in the brush and branches. I suppose it provides some visual cover and protection from the worst of the wind; in any case, he likes it there. We don't know where he goes at night, but it seems likely that he doesn't have a real home. Swell: another cat to feel guilty about.

Apparently he has other venues. Last summer, much to her delight, our neighbor Tara discovered that their crazy dogs had dug a private entrance into her basement. We'd assumed that the house was vacant since then, but learned otherwise last month when some official-looking people went in to inspect the place and emerged soon afterwards, wide-eyed. There is a black cat in there, they said. Could the family have left their cat behind? Natalie and I looked at each other: Tara's black-and-white cat Shorty had escaped during the transition, but we'd found him and helped get him to his new home. Then we remembered the garden cat, and the story of the hole to the basement, and we laughed.

Upon instructions of a hundred generations of Italian women extending back to the Roman Republic, Natalie has placed a cat dish on the back steps. We have tried to feed strays before, but the diners were dissatisfied and took their business elsewhere. But we are redeemed: a substantial depression soon appeared in the mound of brown Purina One kernels appropriated from our two gourmands.

Lest they become bored, those two are served a varied diet of expensive cat foods, all warranted to be low in carbohydrates and formulated to keep elderly indoor cats from turning into furry footballs. But an outdoor cat needs real food, and so we're working through an eighteen-pound sack of Dad's Cat Food, unashamedly filled with nutrition and fats and oils.

We don't know whether our new friend is a he, a she, or transgendered, but upon awakening to tortured wails the other night we became concerned about kittens. Sure enough, there was a large gray cat keeping company with the garden cat, just back from their appointment with the fertility counselor, and it seems probable that one or the other will experience the miracle of birth within nine weeks. We understand about spaying and neutering, but we can't catch them.

It has just turned cold, and we're worried about that, too. We will take care of food, and Nature has provided fur, but cats need shelter, too. Would a cardboard box with a blanket do? Internet sources disagree. So we bought a cushiony foam box-thing intended as an indoor hiding place for bored cats and placed it beneath the back porch. I suppose it'll take him a while to learn that it is not a cat trap.

The sun is bright today, and he is sitting out there among the vines again, composed and withholding comment. We will never admit it, but we are delighted that he has chosen our particular garden.

Rust Rage

Separated from eternal life by a Chinese jack and a thirty-inch length of railroad tie, it was a swell afternoon I spent there beneath the propped-up Geo Metro, lying flat on the concrete garage floor in a rain of rust particles. Eleven salty winters had finally worked their way through the undercoat, and now there is bad rust in the rocker panels, down where they curve beneath the car.

I hail from the shores of Lake Erie, where each year nature and road chemicals use our automobiles to demonstrate that iron in its metallic form is an unhappy element, forced to exist in an unnatural state. But the Lord's children are a stiff-necked people, and so we coat our sculpted sheet steel in layers of paint and tar, hoping to preserve it in a form roughly resembling that of a motor vehicle. The universe replies with a rock to pierce the paint on an inner fender, letting salt-laden slush reach the unsuspecting steel beneath. Rust spreads beneath the paint, stealthy and undetectable, and then we begin exploring sheet-metal welding techniques.

When the first suspicious bubble appears beneath the paint every native son of Cuyahoga County knows instinctively that one poke with a screwdriver will penetrate right through the body panel and probably the frame member beneath. And that's what happened the other day. I consulted the members of the Geo Metro newsgroup, but many are Californians, and many are young. Oh, bad scene, dude, they said. Rust is a killer; your car is doomed.

Well, it's not doomed if you have the Rust Rage of a true 1940's Clevelander. I have sewn Volkswagens together with pop rivets, and there is steel electrical conduit in the frame of my old van. I have learned the techniques of air chisels, fiberglass, rust-neutralizers, cold-galvanizing paint, and the finer vintages of Bondo. I shall never surrender, and neither will anyone else my age.

Initial explorations are performed with a violent device known as a needle scaler, which is an air hammer with steel rods sticking out. You turn on your air compressor (every warrior has one), hold the blunt ends of the 'needles' against a questionable body panel, and pull the trigger. And then, at the rate of 120 blows per minute, you watch a substantial portion of your vehicle dissolve into a cloud of red rust, revealing jagged holes where expensive sheet steel has reverted to ferric oxide and washed down the storm sewer at Sixth and Memorial.

War is declared. The Ministry of Defense brings home a sand-blaster and a fifty-pound sack of ground glass, air hoses are laid out and the battle is joined. Layers of paint and undercoat disappear at the first touch of the nozzle, revealing lace-like steel from which the perfidious rust has been blasted away. Then the liquid potions, elixirs warranted to clean, stabilize, protect, and defend the remaining steel from further insult are applied with brush and spray can. Fifteen bucks a can, but we're operating under emergency appropriations.

After sunset Natalie, quietly emerging from wherever she retreated at the first sounds of combat from the garage, patiently applies Clinque Eye-Makeup Remover to the patches of green Zero-Rust paint on my face. There is fire in my eyes, and rust in my ears, and sand in my nose.

I've got the rocker panels on one side done, and the rest of the car wasn't as bad as I thought. But automotive rust is never cured, only controlled, and semi-annual inspections, with periodic surgeries and chemotherapy will be necessary. It doesn't matter: I'll be out there, slugging away. It is my heritage.

City Resident Sees Threat in Local Climate Change

That first nip in the autumn air always brings special thoughts and memories, dominated principally by the sheer terror of knowing that I am going to freeze to death. Fundamental instincts, honed razor-sharp through years of living in drafty buildings ignored by urban renewal programs, instruct me to seize a newspaper and begin pounding wads of journalism into every conceivable gap around window and door frames. This helps distract me from thinking about the wolves chipping away at my frozen carcass out on the windswept prairie.

Natalie, efficient mother rabbit that she is, greets the season by evaluating her winter outfits, poking through the cedar chest, and calmly lining our burrow with fur pulled from her undercoat. Last night we viewed the Central Ohio Museum of the American Glove and Mitten, gathered from corners of the downstairs closet and laid out on the dinner table. "You wouldn't think that we worried about being cold in the winter," she said, looking for a plastic bag large enough to hold the assemblage.

There is a pair of bright-orange plastic mittens, a souvenir from my years of motorcycle riding through the snows of winter. These worked okay, though I thought a lot about a scheme from a 1957 Popular Science magazine wherein the rider's hands are saved from frostbite because the engine exhaust is piped through the handlebars.

Equally fashionable are my striped Chinese work gloves, stylishly layered over two pairs of knitted brown jersey, price fifty cents. My strategy for last winter was that if the gloves were cheap and ugly enough I would probably never lose them, and I wouldn't feel too bad if I did. The idea seemed to have a certain amount of virtue until I learned why inexpensive work gloves are not recommended for winter wear: when wet, they shrink down to a size more suitable for a raccoon.

It would be simpler if I didn't lose them. My friend Evelyn sees nothing wrong with the time-honored string system, though I suppose it looks odd when you doff your Burberry overcoat in the boardroom and there are your Brooks Brothers kidskin gloves hanging from the sleeves. I am not so encumbered with dignity, so I might try it sometime.

Natalie wears these tiny black leather grandmother gloves* lined with about 0.05 millimeters of unidentified fuzz and then she gripes that her hands get cold. My suggestion that a pair of women's ski gloves might be warmer elicits a sniff unrelated to the weather.

Neither of us has had any luck in the matter of winter hats, either. Anyone who wants to track my wanderings through this great country of ours need only follow a trail of those knitted caps they sell at the grocery store. I lost several each winter until I started wearing my trademark hooded fleece jackets, now purchased by the gross from Unabomber Outfitters. When I wore one of these to Pittsburgh my sister-in-law welcomed me by noting my resemblance to Theodore J. Kaczynski.

Natalie looks charming in hats, but she hates them. She compromises with earmuffs, and wherever she visits during the winter you'll always find nearby a little black purse with two little black gloves neatly encircled by a pair of earmuffs. Her general attitude toward winter is that she dearly misses San Antonio.

We will calm down in a week or so. And I have found that no matter how much Natalie hates winter, she likes having someone to reassure, feed, and guide through to next spring. Once again this season, that seems to be me.

*Objection noted.

Adventures in domestic cuisine: "You're going to *eat* that?"

"I'm sorry," she said as I came in this afternoon. "I thought you'd still be out in the garage while I was eating."

I didn't think I'd said anything, but I suppose I did. It was probably one of those encoded expressions of love that long-married couples use, to wit, a particularly expressive and heartfelt oath reserved for the acrid odor of fried Canadian bacon, a mainstay of one of Natalie's favorite lunches. Suppressing the gag reflex, I assured her that it was perfectly okay, and that as a modern and independent woman she is entitled to have whatever she wants for lunch. Even that.

I doubt that most men really know what their wives eat. I certainly don't. Natalie knows every cookie I swipe, and that my peanut-butter sandwiches must be folded over, but of her diet I know nothing. Sometimes I'll open the refrigerator and find an oddly-shaped module filled with some sort of space food, like hummus or olive paste. Upon inquiry she will assure me that she's been buying this since we lived in Pittsburgh, and that it's perfectly splendid, and would I like to try some. At this I usually render selections from an extensive repertoire of retching noises crafted during my early career as a little brother.

Then again, there's my rhubarb. It has prospered in our garden, but Natalie will have nothing to do with the noble plant, especially in prepared form, and establishment of diplomatic relations in the future seems unlikely.

Fine. I'll make it myself. One evening I harvested some lush stalks, enthusiastically describing to my spouse how the leaves must be discarded because they are poisonous, which was all she had to hear. Placing the chopped stalks in a saucepan with 1 c. water plus 1 c. sugar, I delayed lighting the burner until she went up to bed that evening so she wouldn't be offended by the process.

"I'm giving up," is her usual announcement upon retirement, and on hearing this I covered the pot, put the flame on 'medium,' and sat down to write something or other.

Around 1:00 a.m. I was adding the final touches to a particularly fine phrase when I smelled something and ran for the kitchen. It was the rhubarb, now reduced to fried brown stalks crackling and hissing upon a thick black layer of carbonized sugar. The kitchen was filled with smoke. Hastily doused beneath the kitchen faucet, the saucepan generated clouds of oddly-scented steam that reduced ground visibility to approximately six inches.

Okay, champ, think fast. Open all the windows and grab the big fan from the basement. Prop the storm door open and set the fan on a chair to blow the smoke out. Don't make any noise. I was analyzing the aerodynamics of the problem when I turned around and came face-to-face with Natalie, standing there in her pajamas.

Over the years my beloved has forgiven me for the lame, elaborate ruses I concoct to startle her, for she knows that she, being small, quiet, and with a sweet and open personality, except when it isn't, can easily scare the wits out of me any time she pleases.

And that's what happened. I leaped like a rising trout, there amidst the smoke. "Yaaaa!" I screamed, with sincerity.

Natalie was not nearly as fascinated as I was that the remaining rhubarb tasted like roasted marshmallows. Two days later I cleaned the pan with a wire brush designed for de-carbonizing automobile engines and boiled up a replacement batch.

She peered over the rim of the pan and shuddered. "It's pink and gray and green."

"Want some?" I asked.

Taking refuge in rather small jungles

A thicket is a tangle of trees and brush so thick with vegetation that you can't see into it or out of it. You'll get one wherever you leave a bit of land alone so that any plant which wishes to can take root and grow regardless of aesthetics or local ordinances. So fertile is central Ohio that it takes maybe two growing seasons for young trees and tall grasses to grow high over your head, and if pokeweeds are involved you'll go from zero to invisible within a month. Then you can push your way into the center of your thicket and sit there, cut off from the outside world by its dappled green walls.

There is nowhere more relaxing than the midst of a thicket on a quiet summer day. I love them, but the City of Lancaster does not; unregistered and unregulated vegetation may not flourish within its city limits.

Thickets do not grow in parks. Parks have children, basketball hoops, paths of beaten earth and towering trees spreading high overhead. There is little solitude available, and nowhere to hide. No, you find thickets behind abandoned gas stations, where ailanthus trees have taken root in the oil-soaked Superfund soil to decorate stacks of rusty mufflers with their bright-green jungle foliage.

There are good thickets along train tracks, on railroad property where the city can't mow and the railroad doesn't care to. Trees and brush grow unmolested, shading wildflowers and ferns. They tremble beneath the clatter of the infrequent trains, but no one is there to bother you or the plants, and soon there is just silence once again.

But the best thickets sprout along industrial rivers. They're anchored by ailanthus and willow trees, both scorned by ecologists because these are signs of a disturbed environment, as are the dandelion and milkweed that take root near famously polluted rivers, e.g. the Cuyahoga.

I discovered the industrial thicket when I was 14, the Boy Explorer bicycling his way through the deepest industrial districts of Cleveland. Back in 1960 the Cuyahoga River could run red, or green, or black, depending on what the paint and steel producers were currently pumping into it. To this day nobody knows what's been dumped down there. But nobody lived there, either, so trees took root along the banks, trees that provided shelter for more delicate plants, birds, and the occasional butterfly that flitted among piles of pig iron and the footings of the great bridges that carried trucks and trains high over the oil-slicked water.

Fascinated that nature could come back to reclaim an area so thoroughly given over to the works of man, Kinsler, that weirdest of kids, would go downtown and disappear into one thicket or another. I wisely never told anyone about it, thus avoiding enrollment in an early-intervention program.

Here on East Mulberry Street there are no thickets to hide in. A few years ago I tried cordoning off a small section of our back yard, letting it grow undisturbed. But Natalie kept looking at the Kinsler-Kawheenah National Weed Refuge with growing despair, and a thicket that disturbed her could never offer me any sort of peace. After five weeks I mowed it down.

But it's okay: the four grape vines in the garden have almost enclosed the space over our old cistern. And the morning glories have finally gotten busy and are covering the plastic latticework of the side porch with unlawful leafiness and a daily display of showy flowers. I sit in one or the other, and think about things.

I hope you're enjoying your summer, too.

Maybe the cats will eat them if we don't feed them anything else.

The automatic light fixture on our back porch has given up the last full measure of devotion, and it was dark as we stumbled up the back steps last night. But I could still see her eyes narrow with suspicion: "Is that another zucchini?" she asked, pointing at a cylindrical shape lying in the shadows on the top step, a shape with a long stem hanging off one end.

The object was in fact my old grease gun, temporarily on loan from the truck for the annual restoration of my ancient bicycle. Even as I explained, it was plain that my beloved had lost much of her tolerance for a vegetable with which she shares a common Italian heritage.

They were so tiny, those last two zucchini plants sitting there on the shelf at the Wal-mart Garden Center, and they did not look altogether healthy. But it was already late in the season, so we bought them. I planted them in their little peat pots, taking care this time to cut out the bottoms so that they would know that they had actually been planted, and I ran little drip-irrigation hoses for each, and wished them luck.

But like my equally-determined Natalie, these plants are equipped with an old-world genetic code that does not require luck. Within three weeks they'd sprouted lush jungles of fuzzy dark green leaves the size of bath mats and settled down to their ancestral duty of producing zuccs, as they say in Kroger's produce department.

We hope to become a principal supplier there. Everyone warned me, but I really did not believe in my heart that the fruit of this particular vine could grow so fast. What I do know is that we're pretty well up to maximum zucchini capacity, and it's only July. I like them sautéed in olive oil: it was one of my mother's best dishes, and Natalie's version is even better. But one dinner consumes only a single moderate-sized zucc.

So she experiments with Z.stews, and Z.with pasta, and other Z. remedies from her Italian cookbooks. The oft-suggested zucchini bread is one of those folk breads requiring one-half cup of whatever's in the title role and about three pounds of everything else, plus every cooking utensil in my beloved's kitchen arsenal. I think you could substitute a half-cup of carrots, or bananas, or cranberries, or broccoli and get about the same thing. With the love and competence my spouse applies to the task they are great, but it's an awful lot of work, and the Zucchini Sisters outside in the garden smile at our efforts.

At length we have learned to be vigilant, picking off the tender young fingerlings before they get a chance to grow into something more suitable for carving into a jack o'lantern. Unfortunately Mrs Z. knows this too, so she cleverly hides her young deep within tangles of leaves in dark recesses close to the ground. Nope, nothing today, I say, crawling around on the rain forest floor. But what I thought was a leafy shadow was really the dark-green bulge of yet another child prodigy awaiting discovery. Tomorrow I will find it, grown to the size of the Jolly Green Giant's ottoman, and with a groan load it on the travois for its trip to the vegetable crisper.

No matter. We are city mice, and the idea of growing real food in our own garden still excites us. We know enough of life to never complain about the Lord's bounty: our surplus will go to the neighbors and the church office. Bon appetit.

We Needed A Kitten. Really, We Did.

"Those are my flowers," she said. "Mine. Do you understand? You may not eat my flowers."

Name of suspect: Dr. G. Webster Ocelot. Weight: three pounds. Appearance: striped. Occupation: kitten. And in his three days here he has taken over four lives that seemed pretty complete before he arrived.

Our moribund floor lamp, converted to a 'touch lamp', began flashing wildly as we sat with friends the other night. Investigation revealed that repeated application of kitten paw pads on its old bronze base will rapidly cycle it through various levels of brightness. Tiny paws treading upon her keyboard today have energized Natalie's fancy computer, and it is frantically checking its storage drives for spyware.

This wasn't entirely our fault. We were on our evening walk the other night and we'd almost made it home when stopped by an insistent mewing in the alleyway. From a rustle of undergrowth there appeared a tiny head, followed by a slender body decorated with bold stripes and a black-tipped tail.

Natalie's eyes went wide. She's wanted a kitten for a year now, and the ones born next door proved determinedly wild, ignoring her most patient efforts to lure them. She'd had better luck with the opossum who patronizes our outdoor cat feeder.

"You stay here. I'll get some cat food," she ordered, and sailed off, faster than I've seen her move in a long time. When she returned there was a cat in my lap, one who thought highly of Dad's Original Style Cat Food. We played with him while he ate.

"So now what?" we asked each other. As in so many other important decisions we've made over the years, there was no discussion: we wanted this kitten, and I carried him home.

Remembering about cat diseases, we installed the newcomer in the tiny downstairs bathroom with food, water, a pan of cat litter, and a towel. I tuned a transistor radio to some C&W, propped it on the sink to keep him company, and he went to sleep on his towel.

Natalie says that when you spend a hundred bucks on a cat at the vet, he is definitively yours. Feline leukemia and FIV tests were negative. Parasites have been excised, shots administered, a tentative name bestowed, and Dr. G. Webster Ocelot, named for his curiosity, wise appearance, and spectacular markings lies stretched out asleep on Natalie's chair. That is because he's just spent the last forty-five minutes driving us nuts, climbing up pant legs and batting bits of hardware across the floor, and he is exhausted.

Reaction has not been uniformly positive. Amanda, aka "La Passionata," has retreated beneath the guest-room bed to sulk, occasionally emerging to growl and hiss at this alien creature, who is approximately the size of her head. Shadow, normally the most convivial of cats, has been grudgingly polite, granting a few nose-to-nose inspections even as he noisily asserts his territorial rights. The old cats have been enjoying G. Webster's Nurturing Formula Kitten Chow, which they do not need, while he favors their special geriatric cat food.

He is a fearless kitten, standing unmoved amidst the storm of cat epithets issued by the incumbents. Natalie loves every cat within these precincts equally and liberally, and carefully allocates lap time amongst them. As she reads in bed each evening they stake out territory near her like competing sects at the Church of the Holy Sepulcher.

We are totally distracted with this 48-ounce guy. He purrs loudly at Natalie's touch, and falls asleep in the crook of her arm, and she is just delighted.

I just heard a crash.

The Test Results Indicate That We're Probably Parked on Level 8B.

"Stop it," she hisses, as I lie back on the examination table and try out the stirrups. "I'll bet that place is expensive," I reply, gesturing at the thatched beach hut in the tropical postcard taped to the ceiling above, presumably to distract and soothe the reclining patient. "I could build one of those in our back yard."

Neither of us is getting any younger, and it occurred to me the other day that much of our quality time together consists of expeditions to one medical facility or another. When Natalie goes to her special lady doctor at Ohio State we usually plan a day-long trip to the fabled metropolis, including dinner and a trip to the Wal-mart in Canal Winchester.

She says she takes me along because she worries about getting lost up there in the tangles of the medical center. Though Columbus is an easy city to find one's way around Natalie has never quite mastered it, though she can whip through the three-dimensional maze of her native Pittsburgh like a chipmunk through a woodpile.

And so we trek through parking ramps and pedestrian tunnels, up elevators and down escalators, admiring the dedication of medical workers and thanking good Providence that doctors don't design more buildings than they already do. Even as we spelunk our way down yet another hallway with a locked door at its end, we are grateful that we're healthy enough to have never learned our way around these places.

I receive the usual warning when she gets weighed. "Get lost," quoth my beloved, as she and the nurse look at me with narrowed eyes. "I won't look at how much you weigh," I promise, craning my neck to its limit. "Wow," I add when they record the results. Natalie knows I haven't seen anything, but she gives me a glare on principle.

But they don't throw husbands out of examination rooms anymore, and while we're waiting for the doctor I try to make her laugh. I try out the blood-pressure cuff and see if I can change my blood pressure by tensing my muscles and making faces. Then there's that little peep-hole thing the doctor looks in your eyes with, only I have it turned around the wrong way and temporarily blind myself with the little bright light, which reduces her to hysterics.

The perky young doctor strides in, looking about seventeen years old and trailing an entourage of residents clearly besotted with her. I make panting noises in Natalie's ear. Everyone takes turns watching Natalie swallow water while I gesture behind their backs to see if I can get any to come out of her nose.

Besides company and questionable entertainment, I provide commentary. My spouse doesn't like to talk about herself and, goofball that I may be, I can usually help with the consultation. They know I worry about her.

"You took the scenic route," says the information lady at the fourth lobby we traverse on our way out. It seems that the parking garage and Natalie's clinic are really next door to each other, but we've been making a big circle through every building in the complex. On our way back to investigate this we discover a new way to get lost.

But the car is where we put it, and I drive us to a Chinese restaurant we'd liked once. "So, are you gonna live?" I ask as we pry open fortune cookies. "It says here that most thoughts are only dreams," she replies, "and that my lucky number is 358. Do we need anything at the Kroger?"

How compatibility ensures a successful marriage.

Natalie said that it would make her mother and her sister happy if we got married in her church, so we signed up. But the blessing of the proposed union was something of a stretch for that noble institution, for the wisdom born of two thousand years of knowing better suggested that I wasn't such a hot item and should be viewed with prayerful concern. It was through generosity, reinforced by a reluctance to deal with Natalie on the issue, that they agreed to look into the possibility of a church ceremony.

And so it was that we found ourselves seated in the parsonage at opposite ends of a great quarter-sawn oak table contemplating a standardized test to determine our compatibility, if any. Not counting the Ohio driver's test, we had mistakenly assumed that our advanced age would exempt us from further written examinations.

There were pages of multiple-choice questions, none having to do with stop signs or railroad crossings. How would we behave, they asked, in an external crisis that affected us both? (A) work on it together (B) ignore it (C) let the other one deal with it, or (D) scream out the window.

We, as academics, subscribe to strict ethical standards in test taking. But there wasn't a visible proctor, and it didn't help that we couldn't keep a straight face, for we know each other too well. Matters deteriorated further, and we were soon comparing answers. And laughing.

I think it is significant that nobody changed a single answer based on these exchanges. If we were incompatible, it was best to get a professional opinion, and neither of us has ever been able to convince the other of anything, anyway.

Well, we passed, winning approval from yet another in a chain of institutions stretching back to 1952. But we hope they don't do inspections, because any hint of compatibility is hidden pretty well around here

I noticed the other day that we had two different bottles of dishwashing detergent on the sink, one his, one hers. There are two brands of dental floss, two colors of shampoo, two kinds of pens, two computers with incompatible browsers, two species of mustard, two cultivars of margarine, and two wastebaskets next to the two computers.

There are separate cars and separate laundry, though we have settled on common detergents for washing machine and dishwasher. We share a printer and a cable modem and the bathtub.

The two cats are hers. All cats are hers, she explains, and she is right. Our two furry cultural critics accept my existence with resignation, though the black one endeavors to defend Natalie, taking up a defensive position between us when we're together. He weighs ten pounds, but he is a determined cat.

There are different sodas in the refrigerator. My favored elixir these days is store-brand ginger ale, while hers is some sort of Spirit of the Rain Forest water with Natural Fruit Flavors. It's terrible stuff; barely hissing when you take off the cap.

The freezer is filled with women's food: five-grain bread nuggets and those strange no-calorie fudge bars. Different sorts of cheese lurk in the cheese bin: her Jarlsberg and creamy something, and my bars of store-brand cheddar. She gets ham, I get salami. I am in charge of the mayonnaise, which she loathes but buys me anyway. She is kind enough to keep me from seeing her peanut-butter-and-bananas-on-toast, and she will not begrudge me raw peanuts.

So how compatible is that? If your score is forty or less, find another fiancé, says the quiz in Woman's Day.

A lot they know.

Mystery Couple is Gone, Say Hotel Officials

My Natalie, a noted scholar, is often asked to participate in conferences and seminars, and I am sometimes drafted to keep her company and share the weirder experiences of the journey. This one was to Salt Lake City, where we found ourselves booked into Room 914 of the Little America Hotel.

A visitor to the sort of motel we ordinarily patronize is greeted by a lobby paneled in knotty pine, with a picture of Praying Hands, a stack of pizza coupons, and a rack of color brochures for Luray Caverns. The lobby of the Little America, on the other hand, was clearly commissioned for the Court of Nicholas, Tsar of all the Russias. Elaborate crystal chandeliers hang from the elaborate ceiling high above thick, elaborate carpeting on the marble floor. The marble walls are lined with paintings and gold-encrusted mirrors, and the hallways with marble tables upon which sit Louis XIV urns. Around every corner is a tiny shop selling things like $900 sculptures of clowns or cowboys or fish.

It's not a problem we run into very often, but I think many men my age would agree that compulsory luxury can be just awful. Much to Natalie's distress, I'm not enthusiastic about restaurants, and fancy restaurants are even worse. But these are nothing compared to several nights in a sumptuous hotel. I feel like I've stowed away on an ocean liner. Suspicious hotel detectives scrutinize me. It's Kinsler the Wastrel, lounging in the elaborate Victorian lobby of the great hotel with derby hat, waxed moustache and cigar, even as his picture is prominently displayed alongside newspaper accounts of his dastardly crimes back East.

I had to wait there for Natalie to finish her scholarly work each afternoon, lurking in my gang-warfare hooded sweatshirt and Wal-mart jeans among the fashionable travelers with their designer briefcases and tiny cell phones. Maybe the security people were at a meeting, or perhaps it was my usual ox-like innocence, but nobody ever got around to throwing me out.

I'm sure that those sophisticated guests aren't confused by places like the lobby-level men's room. It was like a mahogany-paneled beach cabana, a row of doors with burnished metal latches. Puzzled, yet driven on by the forces of nature, I gave one a pull and stepped inside a small, enclosed room with a polished brass tissue holder and a chandelier on the ceiling. I felt terribly impolite doing what I did, but there was no choice.

Natalie was entranced with Room 914's bathroom. Two rooms, actually: the dressing room, with its big closet, mirrored sliding doors, a huge sink, and maybe fifty-three drawers built into the wall; and the bathroom proper, with a great oval tub and another sink. Walls and floors were all marble and mirrors, and I kept saying howdy to myself as I took a shower and brushed my teeth.

Each evening we would come in to find that our bed had been turned down, the pillows re-arranged and fluffy terrycloth robes placed at the foot. A kind of chocolate mint that Natalie adores gleamed on each pillow.

Now we are home, where my next project is to construct a temporary shower from a washtub in our chilly downstairs half-bath so we can maintain some level of hygiene when and if we begin to remodel the upstairs one. That bathroom is itself about the size of one of Room 914's closets, and there are no robes or chocolates waiting for her here. But there are cats to welcome us, and I think that if I hold her she might not miss the robe all that much.

Wide Ruled, not College Ruled.

"What do you mean?" asked Natalie, sounding a bit defensive as she rummaged through the eraser bin. "And just what is a 'chubby eraser,' anyway?'"

"You know perfectly well what I mean," I replied from the glue stick display. "The only reason we are here is that we love to buy school supplies. We're hooked."

We thought we were just being charitable: a family near us has more kids than cash, so we're buying their school supplies this year. But it's really just a way to feed our habit.

My beloved and I regularly flunk those magazine quizzes that are supposed to measure a couple's compatibility. Yet we keep discovering common compulsions, one of which starts jungle drums pulsing every August when those black and yellow signs with red apples appear in store windows.

We savor school supplies like fine wine, unable to resist the smell of fresh crayons and yellow pencils, the feel of wide-ruled fillers and crisp spiral notebooks. Our home office looks like the wreck of the good ship Crayola, with pads and pens and markers and notebooks in stacks. At last count we possessed five staplers, and we've just added my father's collection: he loved engineers' pencils, slide rules and graph paper.

And now here we are in Aisle 15, transformed this month into a grotto of three-ring filler paper. To their everlasting credit, our local stores don't seem to make a dime on required school supplies. Those prices have to be well below cost, and it's good business for everyone. But we two, members of the Class of 1965, must pass by these tempting stacks of blank school materials on our way to the pharmacy and the prune juice, and it is wrenching. Hence our largesse to the local kids.

The supply lists are challenging. We held quasi-theological debates over what East Elementary School might conceive to be a "box" of quart-sized Ziploc bags, and how many pencils a "large package" might contain. As it is, our young friends will each begin the academic year with some eighty pencils and six pounds of notebook paper. They will fill five folders and three spiral notebooks, thus considerably exceeding my output through graduate school.

The smallest girl is headed to kindergarten, no supplies required, so we've fashioned her a consolation pack of crayons, markers, a spiral notebook (they're a dime, made in Brazil, for Heaven's sake) and a chunk of notebook paper. We have omitted scissors: "She'll cut her own hair," worried Natalie.

The kid will have plenty to do. Kindergartners today hunker over tiny desks, doing reading and math. "They keep you busy," agreed her older sister, herself going into third grade this year. It all seems a bit frantic: "What's their hurry?" observed my mother, 88. "We took naps and skipped in a circle." True enough: Mom and I shared a kindergarten teacher, Mrs McClellan having dealt with one Vera Goldman in 1924 and me in 1952.

The mild thrill of the new school year is more than habit and tradition. It is optimism: a new school year is a clean slate, or spiral book. It is a season of promise, with all past sins forgiven. Summer was getting old, and there is anticipation in the air. It is delightful to watch kids run through the aisles, picking out the pencils they want. Natalie and I felt the same excitement every year from first grade registration right through our dissertations some forty years later.

We still do. A love of education requires a fundamental faith in human redemption, renewed annually. Happy New School Year, kids.

And Love Still Reigns on East Mulberry Street

It is the Monday after a weekend filled with drama. Natalie's birthday was Friday, and it was a significant one, past which it cannot be said that you've died young. I am four months older, but this is different because it's her.

Thus the day was spent shopping and dining, both of which heal the soul of Woman. Jewelry was involved. Studies have found that the potential lethality of female-spouse birthdays may be substantially reduced if there is a restaurant that the male spouse doesn't understand, and also a large, hushed store containing thick carpets, well-dressed personnel and display cases filled with small glittering items.

Our plans were made more interesting by the latest diplomatic crisis with the cats. The introduction of G. Webster Ocelot, kitten, age 12 wks, into the general population of the institution has not gone so smoothly. The aforementioned creature has taken liberties with the two senior cats here, knowingly and deliberately failing to observe time-honored customs of feline honor and precedence.

Elders are to be worshipped and obeyed. Kittens are not to leap upon the heads of their betters and then scamper beneath the dishwasher beyond reach and chastisement. G. Webster thinks it all a fine game, ignoring possible consequences with the fearlessness of vigorous youth.

We had initially hoped that Shadow, 13, would accept the new acolyte with better humor. Our relationship with him is complex: for several years he has made Chuck, a widower who lives down the street, first among equals on his client list. In fine weather they sit outside, sharing a smoke and discussing matters of the world. In winter they stay inside to eat lunch and watch television. Around sunset each day Natalie's beloved black cat would trot home to sit on our porch until ushered in, fussed over, and fed.

But since the arrival of the small intruder he has been leaving early and returning late. Each night Natalie must walk down to Chuck's darkened porch, calling into the blackness for her cat to forgive her and reveal himself. Presently there comes a grudging cat mutter, and a bit of darkness reluctantly detaches itself and comes to her to be carried home with assurances of continuing love.

Amanda, 10, combines stripes, fluff, and the attitude of an Egyptian princess captured and enslaved. When we can find her at all she'll be sulking on her ironing board in the guest room. The other night, enraged beyond all tolerance, she chased G. Webster into a pile of some of my science museum debris in our office and settled down to wait for him to come out and be slaughtered. The 48-ounce kitten, however, discovered an alternate exit. Padding silently out and around behind our growling, distracted Queen of Sheba, he decided that whatever she was watching must be fascinating, so he nudged in beside her to look into the hole as well. It was like watching a Warner Brothers cartoon.

Natalie tried reasoning with the older cats ("You both were kittens, too.") but the responses to this concerned little but a discussion of the proper presentation of kitten cutlets as entrée or appetizer. She has finally taken to doping the whole crew with our dwindling supply of catnip: as we left for our lethal-birthday celebration there were three furry forms prostrated on the catnip-sprinkled floor.

The birthday was successful, and my beloved looks as young as ever. On our return tonight she opened the front door and there was a kitten reclined serenely on the settee just inside.

"He lives," said Natalie. I believe that may apply to both the kitten and me.

Kinsler and the Lost City of Yard

Every single year the yard and garden get away from us, and it's always a big surprise. We reasoned that since we hadn't gone anywhere this summer, we'd keep up with it. Fat chance: it's become a solid monolith of green leaves. One of these fine mornings I'll be walking out to the garage and there will be a rustle, branches will part, and Tarzan of the Apes himself will stride out from where Natalie's beans are supposed to be, Cheetah the Chimp chattering on his shoulder.

And he'll ask me if I am deliberately trying to grow this new Superfund breed of morning glories, or whether it's just my studied neglect that has yielded a cultivar to seriously challenge Mankind's place upon the planet. Either way, those vines are tough, and they grow fast.

Yesterday I needed a bucket of water to locate multiple holes in a neighborhood kid's bicycle inner tube. I lugged a bucket over to our outside faucet, which was gone. In its place was The Green Mansions, grown over my entire drip-irrigation installation: five hoses, timer, pressure regulator, multiple branch tees, everything. I had to harvest five pounds of vegetation to find the handle and the spout.

A chair I left nearby is now totally entwined, looking like an illustration out of the old Russian folk tale where the old man dozes peacefully, bothering nobody and dreaming of ways to avoid more yard work. Old Uncle Vanya never saw that first morning-glory vine wrap around him, nor the next, or the next, and now he's gone.

Old Uncle Vanya should have dug the bottle of Round-Up out of the garage two weeks ago. The plants were so slow to start this year I thought I wouldn't need it. I kept up with the weeds just fine, even in front. I got busy fixing the car for three days, and suddenly it was The Morning of the Glories on East Mulberry Street.

So this morning I stood, lightly armed upon the field of battle, staring through narrowed eyes at the ominous walls of vegetation. The once-proud House of Black and Decker has suffered in recent years, and our electric string trimmer is the third in a tragic line. The first two fell in the line of duty, each perishing amidst a cloud of acrid smoke as the conquering greenery overloaded their over-rated, under-cooled little motors. A masterpiece of optimistic engineering, our latest machine tries to automatically adjust the length of the whirling trimmer line. Depending on its mood, it will either break the line off short or expel two feet of the stuff to fly off and be entangled in the nearest bush.

But I got the sidewalks edged, marveling at the cleverness with which grass finds ways to propagate itself over solid concrete. Then I attended to the worst of the garden entanglement, discovering two huge melons I forgot we planted. There was a suspended salad where the tomatoes were growing into the asparagus greens. Pushing on into the interior, Ramar of the Jungle discovered two previously-unrecorded trees that had taken root since July, and in wading out to find the big clippers I noted further contributions to the Forests of Kinsler where brave saplings of mulberry, maple and ailanthus had grown to adolescent vigor over the last three weeks. I cannot conceive how even the most destructive Victorian industrial barons ever managed to deforest this place.

But it's done: edged, clipped, mowed, and raked. Pythons no longer hang overhead, no wild pigs cavort in the undergrowth. Natalie will be pleased.

All Work Guaranteed

High on the top shelf in our garage you can still read its reassuring message: "Kinsler Hi-Fi Service. Any Make Stereo Radio Telephone Guitar Amp. Call 363-HIFI." It was the last of my shop signs. There are pictures: "Before" shows a musical eighth-note with an unhappy face, its flagstaff cracked and crooked. "After" shows the same note, happy, with its staff straight and proud.

I spent twenty years fixing them. One of my first customers was Radio Shack #2, their second store in the nation, for whom I disemboweled a shipment of plush-puppy transistor radios and re-soldered the bad connections. The nose was the volume control.

That was when I had my first shop, in an 1880's office building in New Haven. It had an ancient elevator, a cool frosted-glass window in the door and a guy who gave singing lessons downstairs.

But I wanted a shop I could live in, so I moved into an old storefront at 1324½ State Street. It was up the street from the abandoned Gilbert Hall of Science, where Erector Sets were once made. Someone came in to get his fortune told, which is how I learned that the former tenants had been gypsies.

The neighborhood was deteriorating, so I covered over my vulnerable windows with plywood, painted white and adorned with modern-art twelve-inch black letters laid out with compass and ruler. Then someone thought I was an art gallery.

Everything's fun if you're young enough: I installed a gas hot-plate and set up housekeeping in the back room. It was as crude as any retail establishment not built of logs, but I made money repairing the expensive, fragile, and poorly-engineered electronics of the 1970's. Power amplifiers burned up, phonograph motors seized when their feeble British lubricants dried out, and an entire generation of loudspeakers crumbled into dust when the early polyurethane plastic spontaneously deteriorated. I developed a cure for 8-track tape players so they'd play without a paper matchbook wedged beneath the cartridge.

Neighboring buildings had begun to burn around me when I moved to my next shop, an old garage high on a hill overlooking Long Island Sound. Business was good. My sign there was a four-by-eight sheet of plywood, and in the wind that blew straight off the ocean it took me hours to mount it on its tall steel mast along US Route 1. I still have dreams about it.

There was only one door. It opened outward, which was fun when the snow piled against it in a blizzard. And I failed the plumbing test on the 1980 census because I didn't have hot water. But by then I'd finished with my college classes, and I was ready to go off to graduate school.

After Graduate School 1.0 crashed I installed Kinsler Hi-Fi in another New Haven office building, where I lived like an ape in a tree for three more years. Life was made more interesting because there were people in the other offices and the only bathroom was down the hall.

I got another chance at graduate school at the University of Pittsburgh, and re-established Kinsler Hi-Fi one last time at 5131 Penn Avenue in that city, this time with a water heater. But times were changing. By 1986, electronic equipment was much better and far cheaper, and the repair business was dying. Teaching jobs were easier money than turntables, and a short person named Natalie had begun to visit.

I still have my equipment, and spare parts for 1974 cassette recorders. It's all in the garage, where the sign looks down on it and remembers.

The Day the Gypsies Came.

Time smooths off the rough corners of college memories, but even so it is clear that 1965 was a quieter time at Ohio State University. The harsh party culture of today hadn't descended upon the campus, football was not yet a cult, and you couldn't get into much trouble even if you were as clueless as our clan of suburban freshman kids.

I was out buying a slide rule at the Oliver Rexall drug store one afternoon when I saw the groups of small dark-eyed children moving quickly through the crowds on High Street. "Can you do me this one favor, Mister? Mister, Mister, a quarter, Mister!"

There weren't any campus panhandlers then, and I'd never seen any in Cleveland Heights, and I certainly wasn't prepared for child beggars. I thought that maybe they weren't really beggars; maybe a psychology experiment or one of the theater groups I'd heard about. Probably the older students would explain when I got back to the dorm.

But the dorm contained only further mystery. In the crowded lobby, grandly seated by the elevators, was a dark-eyed, middle-aged woman. She wore a headscarf and a flowered dress and had a big tray on her lap filled with beads and trinkets for sale. I just stared. I think everyone else was afraid to do even that, afraid to appear unsophisticated.

But I was a thoughtful lad. I considered the evidence, recalled some of my mother's stories, and finally came to the inescapable if unlikely conclusion that a band of gypsies had descended on 70 W 11th Avenue.

The rest of the innocents in our bunch had independently arrived at the same result. "Okay. Gypsies," quoth the flower of Ohio youth, looking around at one another. "Now what?"

Apparently we were as qualified as anyone to decide that. If the campus police or our dormitory director ever knew what was happening, they never told us.

So we did our best. About all we knew about gypsies was that they had cool music and were supposed to steal things. But the people we'd seen weren't scary or anything, and my roommate, the wise T. Craig Hawkins, observed that no respectable bandit of any stripe would want our stuff. We had engineering textbooks, a transistor radio, two laundry bags, T. Craig's old phonograph, my collection of old bike parts and an institutional-sized glass mayonnaise jar where our goldfish lived.

I suppose that someone, probably our floor director, must have advised us to keep our doors locked and be suspicious of strangers; always good advice for kids who'd left suburban Bucyrus but a few months ago.

So we went to class, and ate, and slept, but it was exciting. The gypsy lady appeared here and there, sort of like a symbol in one of those foreign movies that the art students liked. We gave the kids quarters. T. Craig did a good imitation of them.

A few days later, the gypsies vanished, doubtless disappointed with the pickings available at a school that charged $150.00 per quarter.

They were probably a community of Roma people; one of several bands that my mother says have always roamed Ohio. They are with us still, traveling the interstates in RV's and working as itinerant sheet metal workers—a trade that reflects their traditional work as tinkers who repaired pots and pans in a thriftier age.

The excitement was over, and we missed them. They left us plopped back in Columbus and Chemistry 411, with a quiz on Tuesday.

Maybe the Grim Reaper Can Deal with the Morning Glories While He's Here

"If I never come back, you should just go on without me," she said, packing her suitcase. "The health insurance is paid up for this year, and we're both listed on the bank account. My sister will know what to do about the cemetery."

This is not the sort of thing that a husband hears every day, so I took notice. I knew that part of it was the date, September 11, which always bothers her. And she was going to be gone overnight, staying with friends in Athens to avoid a late night drive back home, and she hates it.

I looked into her eyes and asked that question that means so much to long-time lovers and companions: "What the heck is the matter with you? And can I get rid of the cats after you cash in?"

She gave me a look. "I'm just feeling gloomy. I was up late reading last night. One of the women in my book died, and it was horrible."

"Went down in a hail of Spanish gunfire, eh?" I ventured, receiving another look in return. Natalie reads stories about strong women seeking the truths within their own emotions, or something. I prefer ships and gunfire.

She persisted: "You'll get a life insurance settlement, and you can get a survivor's pension. The lawyer will know what to do."

I held her. "What is with you today?" I asked again. But I knew perfectly well what it was, and she knew I was miserable too. We've been like this ever since we found that, to our mutual dismay, we had become emotionally stuck with each other. We cannot take each other's existence for granted, and every separation, whether for a trip to Malaysia or to Kroger's, is prefaced by what would sound like solemn final farewells to someone normal. I cannot imagine life without Natalie, and to my continuing disbelief she assures me that she'd be lost without me as well, even with all the junk I keep around the house. She says I make her laugh.

It hasn't helped that we've seen our share of deaths lately. Not long ago she announced that she'd bought cemetery plots for us. In the only previous discussions concerning this topic I had suggested renting a post hole digger so that the deceased would occupy minimal space in our garden, well below the frost line. It's considered poor form for one's beloved to be heaved up to the surface at the first thaw.

But I really hadn't given the matter a great deal of thought. I registered as an organ donor long ago, and I signed up in the Willed Body program at Ohio University's anatomy program. Anyone who collects as much scrap as I do understands the value of spare parts, and my parents could at last be proud of their son being accepted to medical school, albeit in freezer wrap. But failing that, it seems that I shall be spending eternity near Natalie's family on a hillside north of Pittsburgh.

And so my beloved went off on her trip, and returned without incident. "You're alive," I noted, taking her suitcase. She elevated her nose, admitting nothing.

We both know that we can't last forever. We have instructed each other that after the inevitable, involuntary separation, the survivor should indeed just go on with life, continuing it with someone else whom we can bore with long stories.

But right now Natalie is poking around the kitchen, discussing supper and the tomatoes we just harvested. And that's about as good as it gets.

At Least the Mice Are Gone

"I love feeding the black kittens," she said as we drove along. "Today they got chicken skin."

"I like chicken skin," I observed.

"They like it best when it's cooked and still hot."

"So do I. But I don't get any, anymore."

"That's because I take it off. Kittens don't have to worry about their cholesterol."

"How do you know? They could be lying there with their little feet in the air when we get home."

"Tough. So could you."

Natalie loves our outside cats. There are six of them, a nuclear cat family, each one coal-black, with green eyes and a sweet face. The four kittens are long and thin like their father, Garden Cat, who doesn't observe the usual stereotype of tom cat and has stayed around to raise his little ones. Mother Cat remains beautiful in matronhood, her fluffy black fur bearing orange highlights.   Their kittens, now grown into strong young cats, lurk everywhere: staring at us from our potting table, or collapsed upon each other asleep on the plastic chair I was supposed to have put away months ago. You go out to see if there are still any beans left on the vines, and a bit of the garden is watching you: it's a black kitten, nestled down in the morning glories.

They were this years' summer project. After months of trying, Natalie has today succeeded in making contact with the bravest of the kittens, alternately applying head-scratching and cat treats she purchased for this purpose. The furry family has lately begun to greet me with some enthusiasm as well, for I'm often assigned to deliver the meat tray containing their latest offering, chicken skin or pork trimmings. It is a job I perform with some regret. "It's not for you," warns Natalie.

I really wasn't planning on founding my own ecosystem here in Central Ohio, but yes, we feed them, including at least one opossum. We think there are several: possumae tend to look alike. They seem healthy enough, with big eyes, silly long snouts, black ears and light tan fur that is sleek, for a possum. But though their mothers love them, they're not attractive animals: author Peg Bracken said that the one she found in her closet looked like a collie dog with too many teeth.

Cats and opossums seem at peace with each other, and probably will remain so provided I continue to pour low-priced cat food into the feed pipe of the cat feeder I designed. Two feet of six-inch stovepipe will hold nine pounds, or ½ bag, of cat food, in case you were wondering.

We think that everyone lives beneath the deck of the vacated (permanently, we fear) house next door. There may be a route into its basement from there: the foundation is old, and Tara told me some weeks before she left that their crazy dogs had excavated a tunnel.

So now the responsible Natalie wants me to rent or borrow one of those live traps to capture the cats, one by one, so we can take them to the vet and, lest the Lord increase our flocks sevenfold, have them rendered immune to disease and further reproduction.

The possums are to be left alone: I don't believe there's a population crisis in that sector. It won't be cheap, but she wants to do it, and then we'll try to find homes for everyone.

"I have another idea," I said, gesturing.

"No, you won't. Bang, indeed." she said. "You love them as much as I do."

I shall get the trap tomorrow.

And someone else will get to be the curator of our stuff.

"Someone never cleaned off the spider webs from last year," said she, lugging a box of illuminated plastic pumpkins and an autumn wreath from the attic room this afternoon.

I handed in the Easter decorations, which had been sitting in their JC Penney's bag in the hallway since May, and looked in at our little domestic long-term-storage facility. She's got three red-and-green Christmas crates stashed in there now.

The attic room is built above our kitchen, and we use it to store the collection of seasonal outdoor ornaments required of every homeowner since the ascent of Martha Stewart. It also houses several failed experiments, including the proposed hammock for the office and the wheels for the mobile cat box. It was here in a corner that I found the mailbox that fits those screws on our front porch. The linoleum on the floor dates from the 1930's, and there are hangers and hooks for long-vanished coats. An antique, musty aroma, not unpleasant, is the same that you get elsewhere in the house if you pull an electrical outlet and thus violate the ancient hollows and secret passages in the walls.

You enter our attic room through a small door at the end of our upstairs hallway; a door from which I've removed the one-way latch to prevent the inevitable practical jokes. Step in, and you're back in 1910, reminded once again that nobody really owns an old house. We find artifacts from every past tenant in here, and in a dozen other odd spaces.

Our house is filled with tiny historical museums. Pull down a ceiling light fixture and see layers of paint dating back to the Spanish-American War The attic light has a turn-of-the-century porcelain turn-button snap switch designed at Thomas Edison's lab in Menlo Park, its wiring insulated from the rafters by neat, everlasting white porcelain knobs and tubes. Still within the walls are the three-eighth-inch iron pipes for the gaslights that once flickered in our living room.

The old pencil sharpener in the mud room must have sharpened the #2's for generations of school kids who lived here. Eighteen baby-food jars filled with odd nuts and bolts still hang from the basement rafters, their lids screwed firmly to the old wood. I occasionally borrow a screw from one of them, and I find that I'm uncharacteristically careful to replace everything the way I found it.

Our big two-story garage is a museum, too. I found a sea-horse someone tried to jig-saw out of plywood, part of some long-abandoned project. There was a stack of ancient spare roofing slates, but Tim used them last year to rebuild our roof. On a nail hangs an inexplicable hoop of copper sheet, possibly part of the old cistern. In one corner a good carpenter installed a fine, heavy workbench that I use, and I feel guilty for not keeping it neater.

I was prancing about up in the garage rafters one day when I got caught on a mysterious bare steel wire carefully stapled to a beam. I followed it over to the wall, and then down to a small shelf someone built there. I keep my little radio on that shelf, and the wire dangled just above it.. That's when I realized that the wire was a radio antenna, the sort you needed for an AM radio before internal loop antennas appeared in the 1950's. So that shelf was his radio shelf, too: he'd listen to his 1930's programs while he worked at the fine workbench he built. Sometimes I borrow his bolts from the basement.

I hooked up his antenna, and it works fine.

A Dream is a Wish Your Heart Makes, Gratuity Not Included.

"Welcome to Paradise," read the hotel brochure. We looked at each other and rolled our eyes.

Five days in Paradise, strictly enforced.

"Since this is your trip, I get the side of the bed without the telephone," I told Natalie. But I always get the side of the bed without the telephone, because when Natalie is awakened by the phone at night she responds with a perky, polite 'Hello,' as opposed to my debonair 'whaauugghh?'

This was a business trip, and a tough one. Natalie's academic responsibilities have increased, and she was here at her annual professoring conference to recruit new faculty members for her department at the university. With some thirty candidates to interview in a small hotel room, plus a paper to present at the conference, she'd be lucky to see the sky, much less the attractions surrounding Orlando, Florida. And since I was along as a companion and stretcher-bearer, and being more a fan of Little Lulu than Mickey Mouse, I didn't expect to be enjoying much of the Magic Kingdom myself.

It was fascinating all the same. The décor consists principally of (1) fountains (2) waterfalls (3) palm trees and (4) more palm trees. Dozens of water pumps are hidden in the closely-clipped shrubbery to supply the aquatic wonders and to keep the palm trees watered. Northerners expect to see palm trees when they shell out air fare to Florida, but Orlando is 200 miles north of Miami, where real palm trees grow on their own, and the trees know it. Thus intensive maintenance and occasional replacement is required.

The only path through the multi-building hotel complex was past the gigantic S-shaped pool with its hot tubs, water slide, more palm trees, and incessant reggae music. Dozens of professor candidates wearing black business suits and name tags streamed through on their way to interviews, further enhancing the carefree tropical atmosphere.

I took a walk and discovered central Florida just outside the hotel's hedge. The trees there were southern pines, with straight trunks, curved branches and ten-inch-long needles. And palmettos, like palm trees but short and bushy. There were little piles of sand: the hills of fire ants. Across a barbed wire fence a few non-Disney beef cattle grazed in the brush. Showy dragonflies skimmed over the drainage canals.

But mostly I kept track of Natalie and wrote stuff. Our only leisure opportunities were nocturnal hunts for food in the rented car. It seems that our hotel was located in central Donald Duck County, with nothing but expensive themed restaurants and T-shirt shops within a five-mile radius. I'd almost given up hope of finding civilization until we came upon the blessed, raucous community of Kissimmee, Florida, where humanity still reigns. There were inexpensive motels, a Wal-mart, and attractions like the Congo River Miniature Golf. We ate at a Bob Evans, where before Natalie could stop me I assured the young waitress that we were from Ohio and lived near Bob's compound where he kept his five wives.

The Orlando airport is the only one I've ever seen that's designed for children. The water fountains are eighteen inches high, and the restaurants serve either hamburgers or spaghetti. There is an entire strip-mall of Disney stores in the terminal, and the security lines were filled with excited, costumed children and exhausted parents toting stuffed animals. It looked like everyone else had had a good time, which at our age is good enough for us.

As our airplane circled down to the runway in Columbus we saw the trees blazing their fall colors, and not a palm among them. It's good to be back.

The Guns Have Spoken

It's not often that today's husband sees his beloved peering with leveled gaze along the barrel of a pistol, and when he does he is wise to take notice. Even though the weapon was in fact a green plastic squirt gun, one of six in a plastic bag purchased for two dollars at Wal-mart, and the target in her sights was not me, her sincerity did give me pause.

She is the gentlest of creatures, but her self-control is legendary and her aim steady, the barrel never wavering from its target. It is pointed, as usual, at G. Webster Ocelot, our striped kitten. He has been harassing Shadow, her old and much-loved black cat, and Natalie is determined to put an end to this behavior.

He looks over his shoulder at her with his celebrated "Who, me?" face, and then returns to whapping at the older cat, now retreated onto a chair. Natalie opens fire, first to the heart-lung area, and when G. Webster turns to investigate the source of the sudden moisture, three blasts to the face. He pauses, finally breaking off the attack as she squeezes off a few more rounds of Lancaster Water Division's finest.

The military capabilities of today's thirty-three-cent Chinese plastic squirt gun are impressive. Standing in the dining room, I accurately nailed G. Webster at a range of six paces during an attack upon a sandwich I'd left unattended in the kitchen. We've since placed the red gun in the kitchen and the blue one in the downstairs office, and I've thought of mounting the remaining three in an oak pistol rack like the one I saw on the cover of Gun Digest some years ago.

But while Natalie's self-control is impressive, mine unfortunately is not. She was crouched over tying her sneakers in the kitchen when the first incident of friendly fire occurred. I denied all responsibility, but since nobody else in our little house can operate a squirt gun, and direct observation revealed that I was indeed holding the weapon, my arguments of innocence lacked a certain force of logic. "Just you wait," she said.

Thus far, however, the promised revenge has not been forthcoming, at least not overtly. She is simply too sweet and kind, and she knows I know it. She claims that the dousing I received across the dinner table the other night was merely collateral damage due to my being seated too close to the pie, a pie in which the kitten was showing undue interest. "You were in the way," said Natalie.

The squirt guns were her idea. She has raised some eight kittens in her career thus far and has become a firm believer in the ability of a well-aimed shot of corrective wetness to obtain the attention of an errant feline. The original aqueous armory was collected during her years as an elementary-school teacher, and her cats have always been well-behaved. I suspect her students were as well.

My own behavior is not nearly so meritorious, but I think that she's happy with that. Natalie was raised in a family of sober, hard-working immigrants who didn't allow animals in the house, and their implied requirement that daughters remain silent and unobtrusive until married off seems only to have sharpened that streak of irreverence in her that I cherish. Our visitors here dine amidst impeccable hospitality and manners that come directly from Natalie's mother. But a squirt gun lies ready in a dish nearby to remind the cats of the power of law enforcement, and to remind me of marvelous mind of the wonderful woman I married.

A Promise I Must Keep

Three years ago David M Kinsler, born 1915 in Chicago, died at the nursing home in Cleveland at 89. His earthly remains have resided on a shelf in our office ever since in the gray-painted particle-board box they issued him, his name and dates typewritten on a label pasted to the bottom. With it are his two diplomas from the University of Chicago and a framed certificate from the Cleveland Museum of Art, awarded for a table he built for their arts and crafts contest in 1956.

My father would have scoffed at that box: painted particle board, indeed. Had he known, he'd have taken a plank of curly maple from his collection of fine lumber and built a proper box, with concealed, hand-cut joints and a French-polished finish. It would gleam: nobody could finish wood like that man.

I sure can't. Years of watching him at his workbench and cleaning up wood chips did nothing for my non-existent woodworking skills, and I'm afraid that it is a measure of my father's character that he took considerable satisfaction in this. Brilliant in so many fields, he never gained much emotional maturity, and the thought of being outdone in any endeavor was too much for him to bear.

He needn't have worried in the woodworking division. We have some of his finely-finished pieces, many completed well into his eighties, around the house. They are bittersweet things of beauty, lovingly constructed by a man who savaged anyone who ever got close to him. The furniture I've built tends to lean sideways, supported principally by numerous coats of inexpensive varnish applied in an attempt to disguise defects in materials and workmanship.

D.M. Kinsler began buying woodworking tools from England in the early 1950's. The currency balance back then let you buy a set of fine Marples chisels or Tyzak saws for what I paid for my lowly collection of red-painted Chinese tools.

He built a maple workbench, and an immense tool chest of sycamore and oak. I was eight when I watched him lay out the dovetailed joints with a pencil and saw them out by hand with the confidence that accompanies the gift of craftsmanship. He'd gripe if he had to correct slight misalignments, peeling off a crisp oak chip here and there with a wood chisel honed razor-sharp.

The chest, its chisels, and his workbench are in a U-Haul storage locker. I guess they're mine now. After fifty years the planks in the chest have shrunk, opening a crack he long predicted. But the tools inside are still shiny and sharp, and smell of the oil he applied before wrapping them for storage. The saws, the cutters, and the wooden smoothing planes of golden English beech glow when you lift them out of their cleverly-crafted slots. In some sense, they are the better part of my father, the only way he could deal with the world.

It was the only promise I made to him at the nursing home before he died. He was asleep, knocked out by some treatment they'd given him—or, more likely, a sedative. Otherwise, we'd once again been driven away by the usual storm of invective and ridicule. But the patient nurse told us he was in a final decline, and so while Natalie stood there I said what I had to say: "Put in the good word for us wherever you're going, and I will take care of your tools."

I will put them into good hands, and then we can deal with that gray box. Promise, Dad.

Hard Hats Only Beyond This Point

Level 2 of our little house has been a construction site since last Tuesday. After five years of discussion we have at last commenced Phase I of Operation Enduring Bathtub: she would be off at school for three days, and it was finally time to start rebuilding the bathroom. For weeks the new tub has stood up-ended in its carton in the narrow hallway while its new faucet sat on the sewing machine. We've been tripping over the fancy new curved stainless-steel shower rod for the past year.

When her car disappeared up East Mulberry Street I sighed, went upstairs, and began the demolition. The previous remodeling team had surrounded the tub with Masonite tile board ("Not recommended for shower enclosures.") Water-soaked plaster, teeming with life, oozed forth when I pulled the first of it down.

But the remainder of the walls were still 1885-solid, and forty square feet of two-inch Victorian plaster, its inner layer mixed with horsehair for reinforcement, had to go. Clouds of ancient dust burst forth at each hammer blow. I set our big box fan in the window and saw the white plume of gypsum issuing forth from the side of the house when I went to the garage to fetch a chisel. While country music wailed on the radio the old bathtub filled with debris, to be lugged downstairs one cat-litter bucket at a time.

The phone rang. "How's it going?" asked she from her temporary quarters. Well, we're okay: the old tub's about halfway out. I took digital pictures of the destruction and e-mailed them down to her. Work continued far into the night, and finally the old tub slid over the carpet, around the corner and into milady's boudoir because there was no place else to put it.

Morning surprise: the corners of the new tub were bashed in; I hadn't looked inside the carton before hauling it home and up the narrow stairs. Bring it right back, said the store. You'd be surprised what will fit into a Geo Metro when you're outraged and determined.

The manager found me a new tub, slicing open its coffin for a thorough inspection before he let me go. A kind lady helped me load it into the little car, and when I got it home, evil language aided its progress up the stairs.

Another surprise: one of my denuded walls had never been insulated. I opened it up, producing clouds of dust and a zillion tiny nails, destroying ancient technology in the name of modern living. Batts of pink insulation now cover the work of craftsmen long dead.

The plumbing was interesting because Moen tried to write the instructions for their fancy faucet in a sort of international sign language. I had to make a bracket to lower the shower head: Natalie's just five feet tall, and I missed her even more as I measured the height.

The six sheets of cement backer board weigh 42 pounds each, and I staggered up the stairs with each one. The vapor-barrier was in, and I hope I leveled the tub right, but my efficiency declined each day. Finally the phone rang: "I'm on my way home."

She withheld comment during the tour. I'd tried to clean, but dust, tools and disorder remained everywhere, and I was afraid she'd scream. The bathtub in her bedroom didn't help, nor the blue discount tarpaulin that encloses the prison-camp shower enclosure I improvised.

But faucet, shower and drain are working, and we can take showers within our billowing blue plastic tarp. We should be able to tile next week.

"I love you," she said.

The Fur Trade Returns to Lancaster

The black kittens living under the house next door were six months old, and it was time to get them and their parents to the vet already. Mother Cat, her common-law husband Garden Cat, and Kittens One through Four were to be captured, tested, spayed/neutered, and vaccinated.

So a few weeks ago I bought a "humane trap," which is a cage with a spring-loaded door, and tried it on our three indoor cats. Results weren't encouraging: the two older cats wouldn't go near the thing, and the kitten wasn't heavy enough to operate the treadle when I threw his jingle-ball inside.

But we baited the device with a can of Walt Disney "Aristo-cats" cat food, set it by the back stairs, and went inside. Natalie paced about, worrying over cat injuries, and I had to stand guard at the door to keep her from checking the trap every two minutes. It worked: we got Kittens One and Two to the vet that first day.

Wily hunters that we are, we laid off a day, and then set the trap again. "Ho, fellow trapper," I teased my conflicted spouse. "Hast thy trap tasted kitten this day?"

It had, and Kitten Three went to the vet shortly after. When we opened the trap there, Ms Three shot toward what she assumed was freedom, except that it was really a closed window. We almost caught her when she bounced off the glass, but she had a different agenda and rocketed into the operating room, vaulting over a large, puzzled dog just emerging from anesthesia. The vet staffers finally got her, yowling but unharmed, into the jaws of a mysterious device resembling a combination fish net and lawn chair.

We'd never seen Mother Cat except from afar as she supervised her family, but she must have ignored her better instincts because the next day I found her in the trap, hissing. Upon release within the smallest of the examination rooms the family matriarch demonstrated admirable martial skills, rising five vertical feet and changing direction mid-flight while flailing claws that penetrated even the vet's heavy cat-handling gloves.

Finally the trap yielded Garden Cat, an old friend who'd spent the previous winter with us, mostly in our garden. But he was in tough shape, his coat dull and tongue protruding, and when his tests for FIV and feline leukemia both came back positive we had no choice but to put him down. And we never did capture Kitten Four, who wisely took French leave on seeing the fate of the rest of the clan.

Black cats look pretty much alike, so we had the vet shave the fur off each cat's left front leg so we wouldn't keep trapping and returning the same one. But it wasn't necessary: they were all done the same day, and we came in to retrieve them and pay the bill.

"I need help," announced the head vet tech, and the entire troupe of attractive young women she employs disappeared into the back room. Ten minutes later they emerged, each carrying a neat cardboard box securely taped for shipment and punched with air holes. We loaded the meowing freight into Natalie's car and drove home.

The cats have settled down nicely. I arranged their cardboard boxes underneath our back steps, and Natalie has added towels inside each one for warmth. Three kittens now mob her, hoping for treats and caresses, whenever she walks outside. Their mother glares at them from a distance, but she and her family are healthy, glossy and active, and Natalie theorizes that Mother Cat may actually approve of us after all.

It was supposed to be a fast trip to Columbus

"Since we're up here anyway, I need some comfortable shoes," said she. "And we have to find a present for Elise."

The fiends of the Spanish Inquisition were skilled with their hooks, and the enforcers of Burmese regimes clever with their instruments of split bamboo. And in Franklin County, there's Easton Town Center. It was pointless to protest, and as we approached the retail palaces east of Columbus I just sat there and stared out the window like a bullock on his way to Bay's Fine Meats. "You'll live," Natalie said.

The advantages to being a trailing male at Nordstrom's are (1) there are lots of young women, and (2) nobody expects you to say anything intelligent. If there are other guys present you can join the brotherhood of misery and discuss carburetors or something, but this time I was alone, sitting quietly where assigned. While Natalie poked through the sale racks, the young women gave me the same sort of sultry glances typically reserved for the less-desirable reptiles that might slither into their lives.

This sort of thing has been going on for years, and in self-defense I've gradually begun to participate in the process to avoid boredom and perhaps speed things up a bit. Thus over the course of our relationship I have learned to pick out clothes for Natalie, having partially eliminated that unique mental blind spot I share with most men concerning women's clothing. (M Kinsler Fashion Report: this year's fall clothes are hideous.)

But this time it was shoes, and I'm not much good at those because my beloved has feet of a size better suited for footwear endorsed by Dora the Explorer. I tried to reassure her of my continuing love and support: "You have little teeny tiny feet," I said.

"Sit there," she replied, and I did. She and the salespeople discussed sizes and special orders, and the conversation became fuzzy.

“Wake up,” came a voice from beyond. “You were asleep. I bought my shoes. Let’s go.” Vaguely wondering what those young women might have thought of the bearded derelict snoozing in their store, I staggered to attention and proceeded as ordered.

And so we walked across Easton Town Center, a sort of retail theme park based on the idea that everything would be better if your average American city was completely evacuated and then every building filled with merchandise. There’s a sort of mall in the middle of the complex, with kids lined up to be photographed with a Santa Claus installed in his baronial Christmas castle, a multi-level fantasy that looks like a yuletide makeover of a movie set left over from Ben-Hur. Conveniently located nearby were dozens of tiny stores devoted to organic mustard, to scarves made in Swaziland, to exotic wrist watches. Outside were Brookstone and The Sharper Image, firms calculated to fascinate guys like me. Natalie let me look, but I think I may have outgrown things like clock radios that project stars on the ceiling.

Amidst stores that sell hand-crafted coffee and sweaters made from wool that came from sheep fed exclusively on organic grass we found Talbot’s, where she bought the scarf she wanted. For my patience there and with her shoe shopping Natalie praised me all the way out to the parking lot.

But my thoughts were of the years I’d spent alone, when I would spend any amount of time poking through stores and even shopping malls for lack of anything to do and anyone to do it with. “It is a privilege,” I said, but I’m not sure she understood.

The Call of the Wild

"Am I out of chopped walnuts?" quoth Natalie's muffled voice from the lower shelves of the refrigerator. It was serious: the brownies had to be in the oven before eleven o'clock so they'd be done before our guests arrived for the annual Christmas rout. "I will go to Kroger for you," volunteered the gallant Kinsler.

"Would you? You've got ten minutes. Take the car, and get moving."

I can be efficient when I must, but not this time. For in front of the store stood a band of Charity Newsies, affiliated with this newspaper and accepting donations for our area's less-fortunate. I dropped in a contribution and stopped for a brief hello. Even that would have been okay except that (1) I'd neglected to take my cell phone and (2) one of the Charity Newsies on duty just then was a prominent Lancaster historian.

See, lately I've been helping with a historical 'blog' about Lancaster on the E-G's web page, and it is great fun. But I've only lived here for seven years, and much of that in my usual oblivion. Thus I've lately had to bone up on local history with some intensity, and here was someone I could consult, just for a moment.

Just for a moment, fat chance. I learned a lot about Lancaster, but at the cost of arriving home at 11:20 with a pound of Kroger chopped walnuts and a load of guilt.

For some reason—male pride, I suppose—I did not say why I was late. Here are your walnuts, woman. Do not question the bringer of walnuts.

What made it worse was that Natalie, sweet as she is, indeed did not ask questions. We talked about going out to the restaurant, about Christmas presents, about our friends who were coming over. And I was miserable, and she knew it.

“Okay,” I finally blurted. “I met a guy at Kroger who knows about Lancaster history, and I got distracted. I knew I should have had my phone, and I’m sorry I made everything late.”

She regarded me quietly. “I knew there was something wrong just by looking at you.”

“I’m doomed, aren’t I?” I asked the gods of matrimony, who never answer. “How can I ever have a life of adventure if I can’t even lie to you about a tryst with someone in Kroger’s entranceway, where we discussed the municipal contributions of I.J. Collins?”

In truth, we’re both doomed. Natalie is a more accomplished liar than I am, but she can’t lie to me. Neither of us have had the nerve or inclination to stray, even a bit, even in our hearts, since we met 21 years ago. Now that’s doom.

We’ve discussed this now and again. “I thought that you, at least, would have had some luck,” I said to my beloved. “I mean, really: I can’t lie, but you can. I’d have expected you to show a bit more enterprise.”

“I know,” she answered. “We’ll spend eternity together, in utter faithfulness. But I like you.”

“And I like you. But that’s not the matter at hand. Weren’t we supposed to experience life to the fullest, and all that? All we do is share the funnies when the newspaper comes. That’s real adventure.”

We are the dullest couple on earth. We laugh at each other, gaze into each other’s eyes and generally sicken anyone unfortunate enough to be near us. But it is possible, just possible, that the goal of at least some lives spent in pursuit of adventure is just someone you cannot lie to.

Everyone liked the brownies.

How to Cement Your Relationship, Along With Everything Else in the House.

"They used eighth-inch grout joints," I observed. "So I saw," replied Natalie. "And the tops of the tiles are bullnosed into the wall." We were outside the restrooms at McDonald's, and as anyone who'd ever done such a task could easily tell, we were in the midst of tiling our own bathroom.

It's been a long road, one that started months ago when we realized that almost nobody had tiles we liked. Nowadays everyone wants you to use granite, marble, or tiles from Pompeii. The cheerful old-fashioned 4-by-4 tiles we wanted were from the 1950's, huffed one salesman.

But our house is old and silly-looking, and the bathroom measures five by nine feet. Put marble or granite in there and you might just as well take a shower in Cleopatra's tomb. Five stores later we found what we wanted, finally staggering home with maybe eight hundred pounds of tile in white and cobalt blue.

Then came study and research. The trip to the library yielded three books on tiling, each worse than the last. One left out details. Another was British. And the last was for an old trade school: here's the industrious tiler and his apprentice mixing mortar in the driveway with shovels. By the time we finished our conflicting texts we knew less than when we started.

The articulate and sympathetic Nathan who presides over Aisle 44 (ceramic tiles and installation) at Lowe's recognized the fatal symptoms when we walked in. No, we didn't need the three-part super-grout. No, we didn't need to lay out the walls with a chalk-line like we were building a subway tunnel. Use this tile mastic, use this grout, just follow the instructions, and we'd be fine.

All the same, it was a life changing experience. I set 540 tiles, 104 of which were trimmed to length by Natalie. (Our friend Linda's tile cutting machine currently blocks all but the most determined traffic through our upstairs hallway.) Primitive hand-shaped icons of tile mastic smeared on the back door memorialize a hurried trip to the garage for tools.

Grouting the tiles was a special treat because it is assumed by everyone that you understand how to grout at birth. You smear this sticky paste over the tiles such that it builds up in the joints, and then you neatly and thoroughly wipe off the remainder, ha, ha. When it started to dry on the surface of the tiles faster than I thought it would I panicked, thinking it would harden irrevocably, entombing all. I ran downstairs, dumped the box of junk from beneath our kitchen sink onto the floor and grabbed anything that looked like a pot scrubber. Then came ninety minutes of frantic scrabbling at the tiles before my big discovery, which is that thin grout stays pretty soft.

Probably because nothing in our house is or ever was quite square a few of the tiles don't lie quite flat, and I have had to make some of the joints wider than I'd hoped. And we'll have to wait for the fancy trim pieces to come into the fancy tile place in Columbus: we think they're culturing them inside oysters or something. But I've done the caulking, so we can take real showers tomorrow without blue tarpaulins duct-taped to the walls around the bathtub.

I just went into the bathroom to admire my handiwork, resting my hands on the cool, flat surfaces, admiring the way the deep blue tiles reach around the corner to the shiny white ones. It's just a little bathtub enclosure, certified old-fashioned by qualified designers. But I, Kinsler, built it. And Natalie says she likes it, too.

And the cats are full of glitter.

On the way back from a restaurant date with friends the other night our host narrated as we toured Christmas lights: "Then there was the guy who got the award for the year's worst holiday decorations," he said. "He ran a string of lights from the socket on his porch, and they reached about two-thirds of the way around his front window, and that was it." I silently looked at Natalie, and she looked at me, for this was approximately what we'd done our first year in Lancaster.

Extension cords, money, and ladders were short that year, and it was sleeting. We'd bought a fine string of lights, but there was no outdoor electrical outlet. Nonetheless I ventured out with the ladder and some sheet-rock screws, strung up the lights as best I could amidst the wintry blast, and declared the job complete when frostbite began to set in. The result resembled an attempt to write "Happy Holidays" with red Christmas lights across the front of our house in Urdu script.

Subsequent years brought improvements, though Natalie's plan to mount permanent light-string brackets along our tall, steep roof line was never implemented due to terror on the part of the designated installer. This year we're down to three candy canes along our front path, a red bow for the front door, and Natalie's tree visible through the window.

The rest of our street is more ecclesiastically-correct, with LED light strings and an occasional inflated Homer Simpson Santa Claus, but it's not nearly as spectacular as it once was. Before we bought it, our house competed with its two adjacent neighbors in holiday displays, and for years afterwards our former neighbor created a multi-colored backdrop by shining red and green floodlights onto the blank white side of our house. It looked fine outside, but if you pulled up the shade of Natalie's bedroom window on a December night, green light flooded in like sunrise on the planet Neptune.

And our Odd Lots illuminated candy canes don't work quite right this year, probably because the timer isn't rated for marine applications. Last year I devised a clever weatherproofing scheme, with the timer sealed within a two-liter plastic soda bottle, and I was pleased with my resourcefulness as I laid the waterproof capsule in the shrubbery. At holidays' end it still worked, which was interesting because rainwater dripping along the extension cord had found its way through a leak in the bottle, efficiently filling it and submerging the timer. Judging from its state of corrosion the device must have been soaking there for at least a week, and it hasn't been quite healthy since I dried it out.

But inside our little house is Natalie's realm. Her very name means Christmas, she tells me, and there are Christmas glasses and Yuletide napkin rings. The Christmas china is stacked on the red tablecloth awaiting the next group of guests, and the oven hasn't cooled since November. My beloved's miniature Nativity scene has appeared on the bogus mantel in the living room, and this year's Christmas tree is 6.5 feet tall, pure white and sparkly, with kitten-resistant decorations. Three new Christmas CD's thunder holiday gladness from the old stereo speakers I restored years ago.

The stack of cards grows daily and she is everywhere: telephoning, baking, shopping, and celebrating as exuberantly as her quiet spirit will allow. And so my feeble attempts at outdoor decor seem oddly adequate, for there is so much Christmas inside our house that it leaks out into the rest of the world, pushed onward by my short spouse's enthusiasm and boundless love.

It is a Federal offense to be buried alive in here.

"I think we're both responsible for this," said Natalie as we crouched beneath dripping rocks to climb the twelfth set of slippery, dimly-lit stairs. She was right: I thought she wanted to go on a Christmas trip, and she thought I wanted to, and that's why we were panting with effort some 270 feet underground and slightly less than 40 percent through a rigorous tour of Mammoth Cave.

I should report that despite its leaky basement, Mammoth Cave National Park in western Kentucky is a thoroughly lovely place and at 317 miles from East Mulberry Street is distant enough so you know that you've actually been somewhere. It is also utterly wholesome, with a neatly-kept hotel, a gift shop with local crafts unrelated to moonshining, and a restaurant that serves nothing that kids might actually have to chew. The park teems with immaculately-uniformed park rangers, some of whom are young women. "In your dreams," said Natalie.

The miles of narrow passageways that thread through solid rock 200 feet beneath our modest hotel room suddenly open into towering rooms suitable for concert halls. Waterfalls tumble down vertical hundred-foot shafts lined with gleaming marble. Truck-sized blocks of limestone that peeled off the roof two million years ago still teeter high above. We are the only life there; the millions of bats who once lived there have been gone for a hundred years, victims of tourism. Halfway through the tour, in a dry tunnel, the ranger gathers everyone around, asks for quiet, and turns off the lights. The darkness and silence are impenetrable.

Afterward, outside in the sunny forest, we looked back at the cave entrance we'd come through: an improbable steel door in the side of a hill. Outside, it's Kentucky. Inside, it is pinnacles of rock where dragons ought to live.

Places that abound with natural wonders aren't ordinarily very prosperous, and you can't grow much in the thin, eroded soil of Kentucky's cave country. When people began taking automobile vacations in the '20's, farmers who had caves beneath their land would fight each other for passing tourists. It was a sad spectacle that amused sophisticated writers from New York, and some of that culture still exists long after the caves were bought out by the Federal government to build the national park. I asked our waitress, a local lass with a serene face and a voice like Dolly Parton's, if there might be a strip of businesses with rubber dinosaurs at one end and a sea-shell shop at the other. "That would be Cave City," she said with a soft, charming drawl.

And so it was, complete with tiny amusement parks and the Mammoth Cave Wildlife Museum (they were stuffed.) A faded sign advertised "Floyd Collins Kinfolk." Everyone in town has worked in the caves.

Neither of us is walking real well right now. We thought we were in decent shape, but upon arriving home after the six-hour car trip discovered that yesterday's physical exercise and today's confinement in the automobile had turned us into creaking imitations of our stooped, ape-like ancestors. Add to this that Natalie, at five-feet-zero, had never seriously considered the possibility that she might crack her head a good one upon the stub of a stalactite formed over the eons, and we're convinced that the greatest natural wonder is that we survived at all.

If you go to see a cave by yourself, you go to see the cave. But if you go with someone you love, you go to see if she likes it, and if she still loves you after taking her there.

She claims she does.

More Adventures in Fine Dining

My beloved is busy this week and has abandoned me to my own devices. I have thus been thinking about the two major culinary principles most dear to the single man: (1) if you're hungry enough, you will eat it and (2) nobody has to know what it was or how you made it if you clean the pan and hide the trash.

Now, I lived on my own for a good 25 years before Natalie obtained custody. Kinsler Hi-Fi Service operated out of five different storefronts over that time, and I unlawfully lived inside four of them. Available domestic facilities were refreshingly modest: a hotplate and an all-purpose sink pretty much covered it.

Accordingly, I developed several world-famous recipes within the constraints of extreme frugality and the lack of a refrigerator. There were fried chicken gizzards and hearts ('mostly hearts,' said the label) and fried chicken livers. There were several variations on beans, and Kinsler's Pasta el Supremo: boil the spaghetti, pour out the hot water (the perforated steel bottom plate off an abandoned Kenwood stereo receiver makes an admirable strainer) and add a heavy application of Good Seasons salad dressing, which makes generic tomato sauce tolerable. There were Kinsler Hi-Fries: heat oil in skillet, then add potatoes grated with the sharp cooling slots cut into the Kenwood receiver bottom.

After profits improved my diet did too, because then I could finally afford a tiny refrigerator. I bought a pressure cooker to make beef stew, a major accomplishment on a 750-watt hotplate: it doesn't pay to be in a hurry. I learned to brown the beef chunks and then add carrots, onions and potatoes, which you can wash if you want but it doesn't really matter because the pressure cooker is like an autoclave and kills all bacteria. Dump in everything without any seasonings, clamp on the lid, and it is great.

For libations, there was generic cola or lemonade. It has been noted that anyone can subsist through long periods of negligible income by dining exclusively on spaghetti and lemonade. But some lemonade is rather acidic, and at the cost of severe gastric distress followed by the longest belch in recorded history I learned that this acidity cannot be corrected by the addition of a chemical buffer such as baking soda.

I also discovered that while it's not a bad idea to save the oil in which you have fried potatoes, you shouldn't use it to make Good Seasons salad dressing several months later. A lady I was courting at the time suggested that I save that tip for when I became a celebrity chef.

Food preparation space was limited, mostly because I tend to fill every level surface with junk. My answer to the fifteen-foot granite counter with hand-hammered copper prep sink was a piece of plywood that I'd set atop whatever was on the table. Upon this I could make sandwiches, and when I was done the board went on my lap to serve as a desk. I got two electrical engineering degrees studying this way, and it was in this condition that Natalie discovered me in 1986, finally coaxing me from my primitive existence with shiny glass beads, mirrors, axe-heads, and Italian cooking.

I have adapted: for many years now I have used different towels for dishes and hands, and there is more than one plate. The hard-won refrigerator now chills snacks at Natalie's office in Athens. But sometimes I still cook some of my old stuff, if only to startle her and assure myself that I could readily go back to life on my own.

Fat chance.

A cold night.

The digital thermometer says that the temperature outside has dropped to 9.9 degrees, and we move cautiously, as if the cold has embrittled us along with everything else.

Natalie is worried about the three outside cats. We went out in the gray cold to buy a spare heat lamp for them, and then she fed them canned cat food, a delicacy normally employed to drug the inside cats when guests come for dinner. "The extra calories will help," she said.

There's normally a buzz here on the east side of town on any Saturday night: people getting in and out of cars to deliver pizza and pick up friends, but tonight there's silence; one or two cars in the last half hour. We're quieter too, and hungrier, eating with heartier appetites than usual. Our gas furnace keeps up as best it can: despite new doors, windows and the 1700 pounds of insulation we blew into the walls a few years ago, ours is an old and determinedly-drafty house. There is a spare furnace blower downstairs, and an extra thermocouple for the pilot light.

We both have work to do, but it's growing dark already, this late afternoon, and the best either of us can do is to take a nap together, lying face-to-face, listening to the furnace and the quiet outside. I try to calm Natalie down. It is scary, this cold, but it's healthy as well, I tell her. "This will kill off the worst of the garden pests, and there aren't any fire ants because the soil freezes."

"I could live with the fire ants," she replies. "I just hate it when it gets cold. Feel my fingers." I let out a yelp as she applies The Brass Fingers of Death to my body. And her nose is colder. "See?" she insists. "And just why are you so warm?"

I make up something about the eternal fires of unquenched artistic passion that burn within me, eliciting a rude noise from my bunkmate. She's still worried about the outside cats. Could they, she asks, gradually adapt as the weather got colder? Could people? I reply that birds and animals have been living around here for thousands of years, and that the Seneca Indians did fine, too, even without electric blankets. It's not clear when I became an expert on bio-climatics, but she settles down.

Morning: she's up, bustling about, getting ready to go to church. Even with the aquarium air bubbler I installed, the water in the outside cats' water bowl has frozen over. Two shattered plastic water dishes taught me to not beat on the ice, so I pour in a flagon of hot water from the kitchen sink. The young cats scamper about, seemingly unaffected by the cold, their black fur thick and glossy. They're eating a lot and I must refill their feeder. The sun is out, and I believe that all of us will survive.

Last night while we were lying there Natalie asked me about homeless people: she couldn't imagine being homeless. I can, I said. I've been close to it, though my firm middle-class instincts have dictated a lifestyle with minimal adventure. But I understand the desire of the homeless to be left alone, with no rules to follow, and some of the sacrifices you make to achieve this. I could always go back on the road, I told her. There's something appealing about the challenge of living nowhere, and on nothing.

She took my hand and tucked it under her. "Your home is here, with me," she said, and went to sleep.

The patient in Room 1 requires attention.

The three cats are in attendance on her bed, and all leaves are canceled, for my Natalie is sick.

She came in sniffling Friday evening after a long day of meetings and a snowy ride home just in time to meet our dinner guests. She endured with her usual flawless poise and kindness, only an increasingly-creaky voice betraying the other gathering she was hosting, this one attended by a growing colony of the year's worst upper-respiratory viruses. When afterward she began to dither about like she does when she feels rotten, I seized my short spouse and marched her upstairs to bed, where she stayed for nine hours.

But my beloved follows her family's traditional sick-and-personal-leave policy which, briefly stated, is that the crops must be harvested or the children will starve this winter. And so she periodically lurches from her sick-bed into flurries of domestic activity. "I will make chicken soup," she announced, this being the most efficient path to recovery. No, not Campbell's: I was dispatched to Kroger for the required chicken and vegetables.

Did I ever mention that Natalie's father was once an Army cook? Down came our giant vat of a stock pot, and in went chicken backs to be boiled down and sent through multiple stages of ritual purification. "Strain it again," she ordered, pointing to some invisible contaminant in the broth. "I don't want that stuff in there." It looked fine to me, but I strained it again. "And I know I'm being fussy," she added.

I pushed her back upstairs for some cold medication and a nap. She re-appeared for some soup, her voice nearly gone, and retreated carrying her 18th-century British spy novel. Three cats, always present when she gets sick, gathered at her feet while I leered at the young woman pictured on the dust jacket. "Any good parts in that?" I asked. She worked on one of the store-brand cough drops I'd bought and looked at me. Then she was gone again, leaving me napping while she popped downstairs to wash the tablecloth from our dinner party.

"I hate being sick," she pouted. She's the world's worst patient, and she knows it. I took her temperature: 99.3, high for her. I've been alternating her on ibuprofen and acetaminophen every two hours, and encouraging her to drink water, which must be kept out of reach of the feline nursing staff.

I never realize how much I depend upon Natalie's steady habits to regulate my own life unless and until she's out of commission, which is why I found myself in the grocery store at 2 a.m. purchasing cat food, acceptable cough drops, and a requested bottle of Sprite Zero, a new soft drink she likes that sounds like a World War II fighter plane.

Morning: her temperature was up to 100, her cough was worse, and for the first time in years she will miss a teaching day. I retrieved the soup from the garage, where we placed it to cool down overnight. Further purification was required, and then it was decanted into storage containers.

Now she has to change the bed sheets, and in the guest room, too. "Yes, and let's paint the upstairs hallway," I suggest. "Sit here and let me do the sheets." She sinks down exhausted in the bedroom chair to watch, too weak to protest my liberal interpretation of the hospital square corner, though she waves an arm feebly at a particularly imperfect one. I correct it and she crawls into bed. "Thank you," she says, settling in. "I'll get better soon."

And You Call That Finished?

Independent research has determined that every man who holds a snow shovel hears the voice of his father. The elder's assessment of the job underway is not favorable: every man thinks his father demands a perfect snow-removal job, and he can recall no occasion in which his father failed to perform one.

You can tell a lot about a man's personality and personal psychology by the way he shovels snow, and mine does not fall into category A. Other men do a proper job, the kind of job that my father, dead these past four years, continues to nag me about over my shoulder: snow shall be removed up to the boundaries of the pavement, anti-ice compound shall be evenly spread, and all ice shall be chipped from the steps. But I am a one-shovel-width guy: the unfortunate pedestrian who finds himself trudging past our house must exercise concentration and agility to negotiate his way along the narrow, randomly winding pathway I've carved through the drifts.

I know snow. Glen Allen Drive extends down a ridge in Cleveland Heights 200 miles north of Lancaster, and you can see Lake Erie. It meant that any chill wind from Canada had plenty of time to pick up moisture from the lake and then dump it, by the foot and in crystalline form, upon our driveway. The snowstorms gave my father a chance to shine, for he had a Gravely tractor with a four-foot snowplow blade. He'd plow out our driveway, and then our neighbors', unasked, while white flames coughed eight inches out of the Gravely's muffler into the chill air.

And yes: now that I've found myself lord of a manor large enough to warrant the purchase of a snow shovel I indeed make sure that I clear the sidewalk up to Maple Street and down to at least Mrs. Arnold's house, because that's what my father taught me to do, even as he tells me that the job is pathetic and indicative of fundamental inadequacies. But Natalie is tolerant, and coos with gratitude as I clomp back into the house.

A wise acquaintance tells me that every young boy is strongly influenced by his father, and that each of us looks to the old guy to learn how a man should act in any situation. I certainly did: David M Kinsler taught me to keep the lawnmower sharp, to shovel the other guy's driveway, to keep all the instructions in a file drawer and to oil electric fans every three months. He taught me to respect the intellect of women, the skills of craftsmen and the authority of the law.

But he also taught me, by example, to issue lengthy criticisms of everything and anyone, and on every possible occasion. This I learned early and well, and so skillfully do I imitate my father's corrosive behavior that if Natalie is not there to help I never know the damage I've caused until I've lost a friend, or gotten fired.

To my infinite good fortune, Natalie is as immune to my bad behavior as she was to my father's, and so I am still married. And if you drive down East Mulberry Street today you'll find every guy on our block bent over a snow shovel, with his father supervising the work invisibly but effectively within his head. I'll be with them, similarly burdened.

But when I put down the shovel and go inside, DM Kinsler's icy ghost does not follow. For our house is guarded by Natalie, whose love melts away the chilliest spirit even on this coldest of days.

Ingredients: Essence of Olive, Extract of Cocoa, Oil of Iris, and Eye of Newt.

All I can think of is that women must teach each other this stuff. Or maybe there's a secret trade-school that issues a twelve-week certificate. However she learned it, it's pretty clear that the procedures my beloved undertakes at her dressing table mirror each morning are far more complex than anything I've ever learned to do, including laying tile and solving electric power system equations.

The drawers are filled with tiny bottles, each with a little brush or sponge or applicator. There are tubes of emollients and jars of exfoliators. A reading of the labels reveals nothing to the layman: when my hands were cracked from handling tile grout last month I asked for some hand cream. Out of a half-dozen different jars Natalie picked two, leaving me to choose between Raintree Eternal Youth Gel and Nature's Organic Bounty Laving Cream.

You'd think I'd know my way around this stuff by now, for my daily search for the toothpaste takes me through that portion of milady's beauty product inventory currently housed in our medicine cabinet. It is a large medicine cabinet for an old house, with nine big shelves, of which my allocation is 0.02. I am advised that I'm lucky to have this much room; other men have to keep their stuff in their Army-issued olive-drab toiletry kit.

There seem to be three major divisions of Woman Products: skin-care, powders/paints/sealants, and hair stuff. Plugged into Natalie's power strip is a hair dryer like Captain Video's secret ray gun, with a weird ionic diffuser to radiate happiness upon her scalp, and a curling iron, and a mirror that lights up with four different shades of light: Daylight, Office, Night-time, and Arc-Welding Shop. And I forgot about the three kinds of shampoo she uses.

The other day she hauled me to Elder-Beerman's Clinique counter to keep her company while she made up an industrial-sized order of whatever it is they sell there. During the negotiations I sat in one of those makeup chairs, reading the strange labels and leering at females. At least they give you a place to sit: over the years I've logged enough time on those stools that I could have earned my instrument rating by now.

I really think there must be cosmetic industry working groups, like the guys who revise the National Electrical Code every year. For example, in Natalie's beauty arsenal you'll find a fearsome-looking device, nickel-plated, with two handles and looking like it came from the amputation kit of a 19th-century naval surgeon. It is, in fact, an eyelash curler: someone must have issued a revised standard stating that eyelashes shall be curled each day to a minimum radius of 0.66cm. Natalie points out with considerable unhappiness that while I possess excellent dark curly eyelashes, hers are light-brown and straight. We discussed this during our last trip when I found her curling her eyelashes in preparation for a long hike through Mammoth Cave. As might be expected, she ignored me.

But I have no complaints. While I still maintain that she needs none of this stuff, it is apparent that with her southern Italian DNA both physical and spiritual, Natalie generally looks younger than the crisp white-jacketed women behind the make-up counter. Despite years dealing with me, she has yet to acquire the grizzledness of women half her age. Women notice this, and probably don't appreciate it, but I certainly do.

Or at least I did. Lately, much to my horror and the vast amusement of the ladies, these places have begun to sell cosmetics for men.

"How about a makeover?" suggested Natalie.

I think I see a mirage in the hall closet.

The scientific principle here is that 100 cubic feet of cold winter air holds very little water vapor. And if you heat up that cold dry air in your furnace—a custom popular with those of us who don't wish to freeze to death—you get 100 cubic feet of warm, exceedingly dry air, and Natalie gripes that her cuticles are falling off.

The Wal-mart humidity meter in our home office reads 25%, equivalent to the Sahara Desert. Thus the electricity between my beloved and I comes packaged in 15-kilovolt discharges that snap between us when we touch. The crack in the old wooden bathroom door has opened up again, the computer's trackball is too slippery to use, and the cats look like they've gone through the fluff-dry cycle.

God knows we've tried, but every humidifier we've ever had has died a horrible death, encased in lime deposits. That's because Lancaster's water, perfectly fine and excellent to drink, has a mineral content suitable for an Austrian health spa.

Our first whole-house humidifier resembled the insides of a player piano, with a big foam-plastic drum rotated by a tiny motor through a dish of water. It was all enclosed in a shiny stainless-steel case with a little window through which you could watch the drum turn when there wasn't anything good on TV. The idea was that hot, dry air from the furnace would blow through the water-soaked foam plastic drum and become saturated with the life-giving fluid, the vapors of which would waft up the ductwork and prevent Natalie's skin from falling to the floor in flakes.

So I put in the humidistat, the power transformer, the water line, and the extra air duct and cranked it up. It helped, somewhat, so we retired the old ultrasonic humidifier that used to sit in Natalie's room and create clouds of dust.

I really did my best with that rotating-drum humidifier, removing pounds of encrustations, replacing the foam, and fooling with the little float valve until I could clean it by feel. When we visited

Mammoth Cave not long ago it took me a moment to realize why the ancient gypsum formations looked so familiar. Theirs were deposited over the course of eons upon the walls of the cave. Ours, essentially identical, formed every three weeks inside the humidifier in the basement.

Finally the float valve gave up completely, flooding the basement. The manufacturer's name was lost under layers of stalactite.

So we bought a new humidifier, warranted immune to mineral deposits. By the time I re-designed its electronic controls so they actually functioned I had a lawn chair set up at the Ohio Humidifier Observation Center next to the furnace. It really ought to work better: lots of water flushes deposits from the evaporating pad down the drain, but so little gets into the air that upstairs it's still like the dryers in King Faisal's Laundromat.

Last night things got so bad that we dug out the old ultrasonic humidifier. It ran fine until ten o'clock, when the little ceramic disk that vibrates the water into fog suddenly went to sit at the right hand of the Lord.

Then Natalie wondered if the feeble basement humidifier might get more moisture into the air if we set the furnace blower to run constantly. It worked, sort of: the humidity rose to 30% and the cats crackle less. But I'm still worried: since Natalie knows I've done everything I can, I know she won't complain even as the last of the moisture evaporates from her dessicated tissues.

Now, there's this new kind of humidifier that sprays right into the furnace…

A young couple seems to have gotten into our photo album

Every so often someone asks how I met Natalie. The answer is simple: I got her out of a catalog.

In 1986 the institutions known as 'singles clubs' were at the height of their popularity. There were few computers, so what you'd do is call Mark Miller, who was the owner of Pittsburgh Singles Connection when he wasn't being a poet, and give him six month's dues plus a signed pledge certifying that you weren't married and that you'd behave yourself. Or, if Mark Miller himself happened to bring a tape machine in need of a belt and some cleaning into Kinsler Hi-Fi Service one afternoon, you could ask for a membership instead of payment, which is how I did it.

Shortly thereafter a bundle of hand-typed, mimeographed sheets came in the mail bearing dozens of names. "Sherri, 32, Pittsburgh, 5'3", 120 lbs, nurse, loves dancing, skiing and dogs." And a telephone number. Women received a list of men, each one supplied with an identification number assigned by Mr Miller.

Having long since been tested and found wanting in the specified areas of dancing, skiing and dogs, I tended not to telephone the hypothetical Sherri's, 32, but managed to generate a certain amount of traffic with the others, some of whom I met. And there was one "Natalie," a short graduate student living near the university not far away. She had a sweet voice and a gentle sense of humor.

God only knows what she might have thought as Mr Debonair pulled up to the pre-arranged neutral meeting place, a campus restaurant called C J Barney's, on his bicycle. She claims that she was pleased to see me, which I wonder about.

Anyway, it grew. I taught at a little trade school, and she was a fledgling financial planner. But Pittsburgh was an optimistic and exciting city in the 1980's, and as poor as we were, the two of us owned that town. I'd meet her downtown and we'd get lunch—not at restaurants, but at employee cafeterias high in the office towers of the big corporations headquartered there, because it was cheap and fun. We'd go to the Strip, an old wholesale grocery district, since gentrified, where they still remembered her parents. We explored everywhere, one evening getting locked inside a university art gallery. Each weekend I'd bring tools to repair whatever was wrong in her mother's house that week.

Her mother spoke little English, but Natalie claimed I'd passed the matriarchal muster, plumbing skills aside. Proof came one day when I showed up, as requested, with a 24-inch provolone cheese the size of a Class 3a fire extinguisher from Jimmy's Italian food store. Switching effortlessly into Italian, Natalie told her mother how I'd purchased the cheese the previous day on my way home from school, and how Jimmy himself, whom she'd known since he was too short to see over the counter of the family store, had given me the proper cheese, and how I'd gotten it home on my bike up the hills, and how, to avoid cutting the noble object in half, I'd had to remove the shelves from my little refrigerator so I could stretch it corner-to-corner.

As Natalie translated, there came an odd sound, sort of a hacking. It was her mother, gone into hysterical laughter.

I once asked Natalie exactly why she'd joined the Singles Connection, for she'd paid cash, and money was short. Oh, she said. It was spring, and she wanted to take a break from studying and have fun for a little while.

"For how long?" I asked.

"Oh, six weeks," said she.

The Hallowed Ground Needs Another Shot of Slug Bait.

Though it often results in extra chores for me, my beloved has an inherent sense of order that I've always admired. She understands mysteries like table centerpieces and when to send a card of congratulations or condolence. I know when to back-flush a filter, or lubricate exposed moving parts, but not whether I should invite two or twenty people to dinner, nor what color a rug should be.

Her sense of propriety extends to the disposal of things, which is why our garden has become sort of a domestic gravesite. There are, for instance, the palms. Natalie goes to church each Palm Sunday and brings home a strip of palm leaf. This she tucks behind the frame of 'A Marriage Blessing,' in our dining room, where it's supposed to stay until the Monday before Ash Wednesday, when it will be collected and reduced to the requisite ashes. But her ecclesiastical calendar is incompatible with her academic one: two sections of Principles of Investment meet at the college each Monday, with meetings after that. And so the palm leaf stays on its wall until Natalie asks me to bury it properly.

I venture forth to dig, toting the trusty K-mart shovel and hope that I'm not disturbing some other sacred object. Knotting the springy palm leaf as compactly as possible, I inter it and wonder how much ceremony I should attach to the proceedings. "See ya," I say as I cover it up.

The ashes are supposed to remind us that life is transitory, but I think the flowers that Natalie buys do a good job too. A few days after purchase, when they've turned into frightening biological specimens on stalks, these too must be disposed of, and not in the trash. Throw them in the garden, she orders, and she won't do it herself. The other day I looked out and saw the expanse strewn with enough dead flowers to supply a national cemetery.

This is appropriate, because I've also buried a few of our fellow mammals back there. There was, for instance, a substantial cottontail rabbit dispatched one spring by Shadow, our black cat. He proudly placed the headless creature upon the front porch for our approval, and it was with soundless, spluttering gestures rather than direct verbal orders that I was dispatched unto Flanders Fields to give the remains a decent burial. Out came the faithful shovel, and may the Lord rest his bunny soul.

The gaunt yellow cat who began showing up at our feeder a few weeks back would meow at us, but even Natalie couldn't lure her close enough for inspection. I suppose she was a sick kitty, because one bitterly cold morning I found her unmoving beneath the outside cats' heat lamp. Most cats wake up, annoyed, when you flick their ear, but this one did not, and I found a plastic bag.

"We can put her out for the Tuesday pickup," I said to my spouse. I was rewarded with crisp orders to call the vet and arrange for proper disposal. But when they quoted a fee of fifty bucks, I again took up the shovel, frozen ground or no frozen ground, and went out to the garden. With Natalie safely away at school, I hacked a good-sized cat grave over in the corner by the electric meter and laid yet another of God's creatures to eternal rest.

I don't know just how it is that Natalie always knows the appropriate thing to do, but I'm very glad that she does. Maybe it means that I belong in this world, too.

An Old House Brings Solace

"Work your way out of it," says the coach to the kid in a funk. And that is how men, as a race, tend to approach life's crises. I don't know what women do—I think they have tea sandwiches, committees, and scrapbooks—but when a guy must confront a psychological crisis, his instinct is to pick up a shovel or a paint scraper and work through it.

The principle is a sound one. Dumb, painstaking work, work that demands more from the musculature than the wits, delays or reduces the symptoms of major depression. At least it works for me.

Digging is good if the ground's not frozen. Fairfield County clay chilled below 32°F will turn aside the most determined shovel, but during the spring and summer months of the past few years I've extended my excuse for a back-yard driveway, a fake pavement made of concrete blocks, to a length of some forty feet. Each hollow block must be pounded full of clay, placed in an accurately-dug hole flush with the earth's surface, then stabilized and backfilled. If I'm feeling rotten enough I can inter five blocks in one afternoon before collapsing.

Painting is good, and gluing even better. The remodeling of our bathroom with its 1,000 tiles and multiple new challenges has been good for months of home-brewed psychiatric therapy, especially when I have to let some bit of work set overnight. Approaching each new project with my usual trepidation, I screw up my courage to finally cut the materials. Read the instructions for the tenth time, break open the resin and hardener, mix everything, gloop it on, align, and clamp. Then there's nothing else to do but wait and hope.

And when you've invested such optimism in a glue joint for a towel rack, or in a coat of paint on a new shelf, it turns out that you've also invested that optimism in life in general. No matter what else happens this night, there will be a glue job or that coat of paint to check on in the morning. And when in the morning I find the parts firmly in place, or the paint hard and glossy, there comes the satisfaction of accomplishment. Otherwise there's remediation to be performed, which is okay, because even in the disappointment of the moment scraping ill-cured glue or sanding down the bad part of the paint instantly relieves the mind of more theoretical concerns.

Plumbing repair is also good. New plumbing requires intelligent decisions in cost analysis, styling, execution, and pipe routing. But plumbing repair merely requires that you remove, somehow, the evil corroded pipes and screw in new ones.

Our two toilets must be moved soon, and so in anticipation I am treating them to new flush valves and tank-to-bowl gaskets. It is not an intellectual exercise: I must bail out the tank with a sponge, dive for inaccessible bolts, dig out rotted plumber's putty, scrape everything clean, and replace old parts with identical new ones. And kindly do not over-tighten the bolts or you'll crack the porcelain, you oaf, state the instructions in English and Spanish. I find it impossible to maintain my usual state of depression when wrestling with a pipe wrench.

As I briefly bask in the glow of another completed job I joyfully thrust the encrusted old flush valve near the averted face of my beloved, manipulating the flap valve like a ventriloquist. It congratulates me. The old gloom will catch up with me soon enough, but then there will be more jobs to do.

I think this is why Natalie wanted an old house.

Diminutive Wife Heavily Favored In Contest with Weather

The clatter came from a quarter of our little house that's usually silent, and I was already on my way up when I heard the plaintive cry for assistance. It was my short spouse, who in an attempt to retrieve her daffodil door wreath and string of goofy Easter-egg lights from our little attic room had stranded herself amidst the pieces of a bathroom cabinet I was painting in there.

This is the sort of thing I've learned to expect each March, when all the basic forces of nature converge upon our little household. Winter has turned infinite. (Natalie hates winter.) Spring is supposed to begin, but it doesn't. (Natalie loves spring.) The academic quarter at Ohio University slides into examinations, project presentations, receptions, faculty meetings and then, abruptly, spring break. March 20th is our wedding anniversary, and this year there's an early Easter, an emotional time for anyone with Natalie's level of spiritual devotion.

On our way to have dinner with friends yesterday we stopped to buy a chocolate bunny for their four-year-old, and until I realized that I couldn't extract her from the Easter grotto at Meijer it hadn't occurred to me that my beloved is as vulnerable to Easter as she is to Christmas. There's not as much baking involved, but Easter has more chocolate and more stuffed animals. My job is to take the latter, especially the huge ones, from their various store shelves and hand them to Natalie to be hugged. "I can't take you home now," she says to each, "but if you stay here someone will buy you soon."

Yeah, I said. Where do you think that fake fur they use for coats nowadays comes from? The faux-fur agent comes into the store the night after Easter with his sack and his Dritz seam-ripper, and that's where all the happy bunnies go. She looked at me. "I'll make you buy all the stuffed animals, so they'll be safe."

Energized by the holiday's approach, she bustled off today on an urgent resupply mission, declaring the quest for chocolate eggs on Holy Saturday equivalent to shopping for gifts on Christmas Eve. On her way out she hauled me outside to search for any sign of spring, no matter how obscure. Fortunately the expedition was a success: "There's a crocus!" she cried, and indeed, a yellow-orange bud had poked its way up through our ivy. "My mother used to call them 'Lina's flowers,'" she said, referring to her family's name for her, "because I always made such a big deal when they came up. They mean it might warm up some day."

"I regret to inform you," I told her, "that it is freezing out here. It is, in fact, snowing."

"I don't care. It means there's hope. Let's go, spring!"

But she had to wear her winter coat to Easter services this evening, and griped about it. Bitterly she related how every Easter when she was a kid she was forced to hide her new dress and shoes beneath galoshes and a coat capable of withstanding the fierce Pittsburgh spring. "It was awful," she said.

And so we are working through March. We're not sure which one of us suggested the nutty Japanese steakhouse, but she was happy with our anniversary dinner. I sat obediently beside her at Holy Saturday services, infused with another year's worth of incense and theology.

If everything else works out this week we'll point her car south to see if we can meet spring on its way up. The weather isn't promising, but her faith is strong, extending even to me. Lina's flowers are tough ones indeed.

The House That Would Not Answer the Telephone.

Natalie's strategy for going on trips these days is to book a motel room that is too far away for us to turn back, but close enough so we can get there after a day's worth of deciding whether to go or not. That's how we got to the Fairfield Inn in Charleston, West Virginia the other night, the first stop on our annual southward pilgrimage in search of spring and daffodils.

We'd left bright and early at 5:30 in the evening, having spent the day dithering around the house packing, force-feeding me food left in the refrigerator, wrangling cats, washing clothes, backing up computer files, and generally being ineffective.

You can't see all that much of Charleston in the dark, but guided by the firm, slightly impatient voice of Ms Garmin, the lady who lives inside our GPS device, we were able to ride around and find Natalie's first daffodils illuminated by the streetlights along the Kanawha River. Then back to our little carpeted encampment in Room 314, where we enjoyed our usual exotic night life: checking our e-mail with the free wireless internet and reading the newspapers we'd brought. Natalie talked to her friends via cell phone. And I made a suggestion that taught us more about ourselves than we wanted to learn just then: "How about calling our answering machine?" I murmured from beneath the blankets.

Surprise: no answer. Not ten minutes later, nor an hour later. The phone rang and rang. Nothing.

Maybe the power is out, suggested Natalie. That would do it. Or maybe a cat walked on a switch. Yep. But what we were both really thinking was that maybe there was a pair of copper telephone wires dangling into the burned-out foundation hole of an old house recently gone forever from East Mulberry Street. That would do it, too.

We talked quietly. Well, I suppose the cats got out. They're fairly sensible. Right, I said. Way up there on the common-sense scale, just like us. Nobody could call us if our house burned down except our friends Maggie and John, who wouldn't be there to look after the cats for another day.

And so we silently considered the prospect of life without all our stuff. Do we rebuild, buy the vacant house next door, or take it as a sign from God and just hit the road?

That's where we left matters. Either the house was there or it wasn't, and there wasn't much we could do about it either way. Maybe as you get older you get less panicked about some things, and while I still specialize in panic in all its infinite colors and varieties, like fine wines, I did not suggest calling anyone to check and neither did Natalie.

The next day we were enjoying the sunshine in Charlotte, North Carolina when John called to say that he'd sold our cats to a local restaurant but that otherwise things seemed normal. So the house was there.

Home again. The house was indeed there, and so was the answering machine, paralyzed by some electrical disturbance. As the cats wound their way around our feet, meowing their tales of loneliness and discontent, I pulled out the plug and put it back, and the machine sprang back to life.

I guess we never really thought the house was gone: a disaster of that magnitude would take time to sink in. But the balky answering machine made us think about what is valuable and what is not, for we still had each other, and there were daffodils for Natalie.

Every spring the Algonquins pounded them into a yellow paste for short, crazed spouses.

There are a lot of flags on East Mulberry Street, a neighborhood whose density of flapping heraldry rivals Arlington National Cemetery. Every front yard honors something: the Ohio State Buckeyes, the Pittsburgh Steelers, prisoners of war, the United States of America, Snoopy, or in our particular case, daffodils. But it's been a tough winter: all the flags are a bit faded, and some have suffered major damage. Natalie's best daffodil flag, currently hoisted to its seasonal place of honor on the front porch, looks like it last flew over the Alamo: there are odd longitudinal slits in its Oriental fabric, and the edging has flapped off. We're looking for a new one, but nobody seems to sell garden flags anymore.

She loves daffodils. I've just finished installing her new daffodil tiles in the bathroom—two over the sink and two over the bathtub. She would like a stained-glass daffodil screen to hang over the window in our front hall, and I'm supposed to be looking for daffodil appliqués to somehow appliqué to our kitchen cabinets. For some reason, probably because she hasn't thought of it yet, my beloved hasn't made me plant daffodil bulbs around the vacant house next door; we ran out of space on our side of the property line years ago.

Natalie ignores my detailed descriptions of the Comprehensive State Program for Daffodil Eradication, and knows that there is no such chemical as daffodilicide, and no plans to air-drop it from helicopters, helicopters whose pilots paint yellow flowers impaled upon black X's on their cockpit doors after each mission. In the grocery store she no longer leaps like a rising trout when I breathlessly inform her of a fictitious rack of paper towels or oven mitts emblazoned with daffodils. But she also knows that I look for just such things.

The other day we took a compulsory journey to Athens, down where the weather has been just a bit milder, ostensibly to pick up our tax return from the accountant, but it was really to look at spring flowers. On spring automobile rides I have learned to distinguish gesture/squawk Type A, which means “There is a large truck loaded with locomotive parts bearing down upon us,” from gesture/squawk Type B, which means, “To our right is visible yet another of this year’s 3,100 roadside patches of daffodils.”

Her friends give her things with daffodils on them. There are at least five daffodil mugs in one china cabinet and a huge delicate ceramic daffodil I’m terrified of breaking sitting in the other. There are daffodil plates, and two framed daffodil photographs, one of which is cut from a magazine. (We also have a print of a cardinal cut from some wrapping paper we got, which should illustrate how lavish we’ve been with home décor around here.)

Though they last only a few days (it looks like it may freeze tonight) Natalie remains devoted to her yellow flowers of spring, I prefer things with permanence, like partially-rusted wrenches that I’ll never use, and really cool old bottles. When I go to my reward she will stack them into boxes and return them to their natural habitat at the flea market, where they will generate more wealth when sold to the next generation of men.

But in the meantime she will watch for old boxes of screws I might like and I shall continue to scout for her daffodil towels. The Great Mandala of the Mason Jar of Potentially-Useful Bolts will rotate yet another notch on its axis for me, and the daffodils will bloom as they do every spring. For her.

Duel In the Sun

The grass was getting tall, and it was about time to wake Lazarus the Lawn Mower from his long winter nap for another fun-filled season chopping up food wrappers and getting tangled in string. I poured in some Wal-mart 20W-50, the thickest oil you can buy that doesn't have to be applied with a spatula, and administered a ceremonial shot of promo-grade carb cleaner to dissolve a winter's worth of evaporated gasoline from the carburetor.

Years of uninspired sharpening had sculpted the blade into an abstract, fluid shape, sort of like one of those Arab swords, but it looked like it might still cut grass. So I ran the angle grinder over it again and proceeded to the refueling station, a plastic gas can stored in the back of the truck. There I discovered that God was indeed in His heaven, for the 3.5 HP Briggs and Stratton Sprint E-Z-Pull engine started on the third E-Z pull of the starter cord.

Off I went, turning a spring's worth of grass, weeds, grape-vine clippings, and dried tomato plants into innocent mulch, or at least chips too small to recognize as yard waste. But then I discovered a hitherto-concealed pile of last summer's garden stakes obstructing further progress, so I had to turn off the mower.

Now, stopping Lazarus is an adventure that rivals starting Lazarus. A piece of steel rod salvaged from a tomato cage is pressed firmly onto the mower deck near the spark plug and tilted until it contacts the plug terminal, thus shorting out the spark and initiating a series of agonized gasps and pops, after which the engine may stop. Failure to follow the procedure properly results in an inadvertent and painful circuit that includes the 12,000 volt spark-plug terminal, the operator, and the earth under his feet.

And then Lazarus refused to start again. After five pulls I sprayed in more carb cleaner, and then the forbidden starting ether. The spark plug was fine. Theorizing over the distinctly finite number of things that can go wrong with a one-cylinder lawnmower engine I unbolted the engine lid and at length discovered the deep cut in the spark plug cable insulation: the spark was short-circuiting.

I know I should have fixed this with something better than electrical tape, but I've got a graduate degree in electrical engineering and thus feel that electric currents ought to obey me, and it was getting late. On the second pull Lazarus again coughed to life, expelling dense clouds of hydrocarbons into the atmosphere.

Yay. I was mowing, moving right along past the Rose Bush of Treachery, which grows pink roses and the meanest thorns outside of the Los Nachos National Desert. And then Lazarus stopped. Dead. Dead, and now the starter cord wouldn't pull.

Oh, my gosh: I have somehow seized the piston in the cylinder. I thought about engine reboring and new piston rings as I grabbed the socket wrenches and tore off the engine case again. However, the student should recall that the blade of a standard rotary mower is bolted directly to the engine shaft, and thus any obstruction to the blade—say, a piece of the semi-concealed aluminum lawn edging I once installed along our concrete path—serves as a marvelous imitation of a seized engine when jammed between blade and mower deck.

The engine lid is easy to get on once you've practiced its removal and re-installation for an hour and a half. Lazarus started again as if nothing had happened, and we finished up as the mild April night fell.

"Oh." said Natalie. "You did the lawn. Thank you."

Kinsler, Master of Disguise, Goes Out on the Town.

G Webster Ocelot, professional house cat, sits on the bed wide-eyed with fascination at this fine brightly-colored ribbon-thing flashing before him and takes a couple of trial swipes with a long striped paw. I pause so we can briefly discuss the matter and then resume the task of trying to get my necktie knotted properly, a job I normally don't undertake more than about once a year.

As the end of the school term approaches, so does the season of awards banquets, an international phenomenon in which each trailing spouse of a college faculty member finds himself digging out a suit from the back of a closet. It is my legal duty to show up clipped, clean, suited up and with a proper attitude at the appointed time and place, typically somewhere on the Ohio University campus in Athens. Big universities love awards banquets, and anyone married to a professor can expect to attend several per year.

Natalie loves it when I have to get dressed up and, as women will do, takes a certain measure of additional delight in my general discomfort at the prospect. Ever since I gave up on job interviews The Suit emerges only for these banquets and for funerals, which is why the jacket generally contains a souvenir from whichever mortuary I last visited. I poke around looking for some cheery artifacts but it seems that she has once again edited my pockets, presumably to prevent a repeat of the time I produced a holy card at an inappropriate moment at the dinner table. I still think it was funny.

No, I may not wear any but a white undershirt, there is one on the chair. My red bandanna handkerchief is banned in favor of a tiny white one. No Fruit of the Loom athletic socks, either: she's laid out the black ones next to the dress shoes she made me buy at Nordstrom's.

"The shirts are in their bag from the dry cleaner," she'd instructed, and I pick one out, the collar stiff against a neck accustomed to nothing more rigorous than a T-shirt. The pants are so loose it feels like I'm not wearing any, and they contain weird buttons for suspenders. My customary US Navy web belt is also banned, so I must deal with a stiff leather one which informs me that despite earlier promises I have not lost any weight since our previous encounter.

I don't know how anyone else feels in a seldom-worn suit, but it always makes me feel like the photo caption ought to read, "Defendant Kinsler, at center between officers, attempts to justify his existence to the Court." And he's not having much luck, either. All I can think of is that I'll forget what I'm wearing and decide to adjust the tie rods on the truck.

But the banquet was fine. Everyone in Natalie's world knows me by now and expects me to come in looking like I've just been dressed up for a costume ball, and we catch up with old stories. Suffice it to say that Ohio U's business school has people who are both important and kind. They get through the speeches, including Natalie's, and then we are released. In the parking garage I remove jacket, tie and shirt and proceed in my white undershirt, dress pants and dress shoes, looking like I've just escaped a hotel fire in a 1946 movie. When we arrive home it takes me approximately 0.6 minutes to revert back into native garb.

"Thank you," says Natalie, unnecessarily. "You looked so nice."

The readings seem to indicate signals from Neptune

"I've never slept here without you," lamented my short spouse. You'll be fine, I replied. I'll be gone for exactly eight hours, and I've assigned the cat to take charge of your welfare. "Hmph," she replied.

After many months of an increasingly weird sleep schedule I was finally compelled to undergo a sleep evaluation test, and I suppose I had it coming. When they added up all the naps I took on a typical day it came out to 31.8 hours, and I also seem to have something called restless-leg syndrome. Anyway, nobody gave me a choice, so the other night I reported to the sleep doctor's office at 8:30 p.m. with a Wall Street Journal tote bag containing a book, Natalie's laptop computer, a clean running suit to sleep in, and my nightly illicit candy ration.

They put me into a sort of combination motel and hospital room with a bed, a TV, and lots of wires. As I sat there waiting for something else to happen I dug out the computer and via an illicit wireless connection from somewhere tapped out a furtive note to my beloved that I was safe.

Then Kim, a lady with infinite patience and a twelve-hour overnight shift monitoring people who grunt all night, came in to hook me up to an astonishing array of sensors. Heart monitor, electroencephalogram, a breathing monitor, stuff on my fingers, stuff on my toes, stuff on my ears, stuff on my nose. When she finished with my wiring harness I looked like a bearded circuit board standing in the starting gate at Churchill Downs. And then Kim gave me a sleeping pill, turned off the light and closed the door, leaving me under the observation of a TV camera, a steerable infra-red spotlight, and a crackly two-way speaker so they could hear me snore.

Later they gave me an extra blanket: please don't get up or you'll pull out the plug. No, I don't need the TV, thanks. I settled down and hoped that the sleeping pill might work, which it did not. My legs began aching and kicking, and I tried to think thoughts that might put me to sleep.

Well, not quite any thoughts. While I know that the monitoring instruments cannot read minds, I am male and as such possess a rudimentary central nervous system which doesn't always separate thoughts and reactions so well, and there was that TV camera. So I confined myself to meditations on mechanical devices. It didn't help. The bright side is that I think I've figured out how to power a ten-speed bicycle with a string-trimmer engine through the bike's own gearshift, which should make best advantage of the engine's torque curve, though planetary gears on the shaft might be necessary.

I tossed and turned within the limits allowed by the wires for what felt like hours. Finally I asked for the pair of generic Tylenol I'd brought along (it's good for restless legs.) They must have helped, because I had no idea where I was when Kim woke me at five a.m.

She unhooked me and I gratefully dressed and filled out some forms. Apparently the sleep doctors don't hold a morning flag-raising ceremony or anything for their nightly campers, so I just walked out through the darkened lobby, found the car and headed home.

Natalie's alarm clock was ringing upstairs when I let myself in through the kitchen, so I made her coffee and brought it up to the bathroom, handing the mug in through the shower curtain like always. "Oh, thank you," she said over the noise of the water. "I missed you."

Another woman in my life packs up to leave

We come into this world without possessions and exit it the same way. At the end of his life my father had a pair of eyeglasses, a hearing aid, and a ring. The ring went into Natalie's jewelry box, the glasses to the Lions Club, and the hearing aid to House of Hearing over on East Main Street, which can maybe use the parts.

And now my mother is divesting as well. Her mind is as sound as it ever was, but at 89 Vera G Kinsler needs a higher level of care than her assisted living facility can provide, so she's transferring to the nursing home in the same complex up in Cleveland. She's outlived every friend and relative in the county but won't move near us: at this stage of her life she's not about to finish it out in the sticks.

So we drove up the other day to help her sort through her stuff, because she'll only have a single room in the nursing facility. Eight hours of driving for a three-hour visit, but it's a long three hours.

She sits staring bleakly into the future, terrified. How did she get so old, how did she wind up this way, she demands. I shrug, wondering how I suddenly became a font of such wisdom, but she's always asked me rhetorical questions. I was in second grade in 1954 when she solemnly confided to me that as a woman of 35 she'd done everything she was ever going to accomplish. I think I shrugged then, too.

I suppose she expected that time, age, marriage and children would somehow relieve the depression she'd suffered all her life. Even after it was clear that the plan didn't work we continued to hang around, a souvenir of miscalculation.

Anyway, here is the old maple chest of drawers, the unabridged dictionary still on top. The office supplies I'd forage for are still in there, dried rubber bands around bundles of pencils from long-vanished Cleveland businesses, the smell of cedar shavings and carbon paper infused into the wood forever. Here is the metal Louis Sherry candy box that she kept buttons in. Briefly unattended, the infant gourmand M Kinsler emptied it one afternoon, devouring his mother's entire supply of spare buttons, later recovered and sterilized. I'm keeping the box.

In the Roma Wine crate resides forty pounds of amusing yet sophisticated brass animal paperweights I used to play with. Two cartons contain vases and jars she used for her flower arranging, and others brim with needlework patterns and supplies. There's a tote bag full of costume jewelry and a closet of sweaters. There are no family photographs or mementos; my mother thought her destiny was to be a writer and sophisticated social critic, but then these kids came along. Like it or not, she needs us now, and we in turn must weather her alternate bewilderment and fury at the present predicament.

Get rid of it all, commands my mother. And so a friend who makes costumes can use the sewing machine and the needlepoint supplies, and maybe I'll set up a stand at the Old Shoe Factory to get rid of the rest. eBay is proving more trouble than it's worth and we don't plan to get rich on my mother's stuff anyway. We're selling out to the bare walls; our loss is your gain.

We load everything into Natalie's Honda Accord and steer south on I-271 toward home, adults once more. Old adults, who also wonder why things turned out the way they did. Very thankful old adults.

"Let's have some dinner," says Natalie.

Each time she goes away the garden gets bigger.

I get jumpier as the afternoon wears on. Natalie is finally coming home today, maybe within the hour if things go smoothly. It's been four days, a social trip to visit friends and relations and to set foot upon the soil of her native Pittsburgh, required at least once per annum by some Western Pennsylvania Code of Loyalty. She says she had a good time.

Things haven't been as joyous here on East Mulberry Street. This morning I realized that my spouse had been away too long when I found myself seriously contemplating whether to learn to play the ukulele. I read weird stuff when she's gone, and there's a whole page of the instruments in my reproduction copy of the 1927 Sears catalog, surrounded by pictures of 1920's people playing ukuleles and looking a lot happier than I was right then.

The youngest cat, who can generally be found in Natalie's lap, is driving me crazy, constantly wanting to be picked up and held but never satisfied. Without Natalie to sleep alongside the felines have been restless at night: this morning the hair-catcher from the bathtub drain lay at the bottom of the stairs, and what looked like a deceased mouse in the middle of her untouched bed turned out to be a stainless-steel pan scrubber from the kitchen.

I am beginning to learn how our local ecology is related to Natalie's trips. Every spring when she goes off to visit her sister I take the opportunity to clear and lay out the garden and, deprived of her moderating influence, extend it slightly. This afternoon I headed out to get more anti-weed cloth and upon looking out upon the acreage realized that we now have room for a fine stand of winter wheat. Unless we hire a farm hand we may have to observe Scriptural directives on letting part of the land lie fallow, which will not please the Fairfield County code enforcement office. They follow New Testament tastes in land usage and approve mainly of closely-clipped lawn.

The phone rings: she's at a rest stop on I-70, and Ms Garmin, the lady who lives in the GPS device, has issued an ETA of 90 minutes. I've already cleaned up the kitchen, disposed of incriminating dietary evidence, and taken out the accumulated trash, and so I search for silly things on the computer and try not to think too hard.

Another call: she has stopped for coffee and just turned off I-70 on to Route 37 for seventeen miles of rural driving calculated to remind us of what US33 was like before they improved it. Okay, I tell her, envisioning careening SUV's filled with inebriated revelers. Don't talk: just drive. Everyone's crazy out there. Go slow. If she goes slow, I muse silently, she might be able to swerve from the path of deer, brainless teenagers and improperly-secured horse trailers

I long for her to come bustling in, flushed from her adventure and trailing the excitement of the open road. Cats will gambol around her feet. I'll unload the car and steer her upstairs to change her clothes, because she won't begin to relax until she does that. Then she will sit and read four days' worth of comics from two different newspapers while I just sort of look at her for a while, getting used to a house no longer silent and empty.

Update: It's the phone again, and a small voice reports that one (1) wife sits exhausted in a red automobile in front of the house, and please come help. She is home.

Kinsler, of the Fairfield County Paparazzi

The gymnasium was almost silent as the principal welcomed everyone to the commencement at the rural high school last week. He could not know that his school had drawn the 2008 Golden Short Straw and that press coverage had been assigned to M Kinsler, founder of the point-and-hope school of photojournalism.

I am not a confident reporter. I had come in by the front entrance only a few moments before, carrying my clipboard and looking like a dazed fire inspector. The lady who greeted the pedestrian traffic had to gently rotate me until I was pointing toward the gym where the festivities were taking place. I commended my soul to the Almighty and hiked toward the general direction of the noise.

I wasn't sure what to take pictures of. There were rows of students sitting in their mortarboards, and rows of dignitaries being dignified on the platform. And so I concentrated on small details: the kids who handed a rose to each graduate, the concentration shown by each girl as she gracefully negotiated the rickety wooden stairs to the stage in her high heels and long gown, and the farewell that the principal gave to every student who exited the platform.

And they would have been swell pictures if I hadn't been using the elderly digital camera I bought at Target to take pictures for eBay. It's normally a great camera, but contains a built-in time machine: you look through the viewfinder at whatever you want to take a picture of, push the button, and eventually, after the camera finally wakes up and decides to work, you get a picture of what everything looked like five seconds later. And so I got pictures of young women already at the top of the stairs, and the principal looking at the retreating back of each exiting student. When I tried to take pictures of people photographing their kids, my camera's internal artistic advisory committee took so much time voting on whether it liked the shot that by the time it came to a decision and issued its simulated shutter click there was only empty space.

Meanwhile, I wasn't exactly invisible myself. I don't know how many family photo albums I'm now immortalized in, but I really did try to stay out of the viewfinder of the professional photographer the school hired to take official pictures of their event, even as we continued to waltz into each other there in the gym.

But it was a charming ceremony. The parents burst with pride at their kids and took picture after picture. Great-grandparents beamed from wheelchairs and walkers. It is a school where the teachers like the kids, and the students know the principal and the principal cares about each one. This fascinates me because years ago in the Legendary Cleveland Heights Schools we only saw our principal at school assemblies at which he issued stern warnings concerning discipline, behavior, and severe character deficiencies that he would be forced to record in all of our permanent records.

Perhaps I got his message at last, because during the speeches I was leaning against the wall behind the band and found myself distracted by the amazing variety of strange noisemakers carefully laid out by the percussion players. I instinctively reached out to give one a shake, but something resembling self-control somehow gained preference and I stopped myself.

I'm afraid that some pictures turned out a bit shaky: I clearly need some sort of a tripod. But I hope they show how happy and hopeful everyone was on that lovely Sunday afternoon, and your photojournalist wishes you the best of luck in life.

Harvest time comes in June around here.

"I was afraid I'd do something like this," came a voice from the kitchen. "There were two white bowls of cut-up red things, and I put the garlic slices in the wrong one."

The right one was the tomato salad. The wrong one was the strawberries.

"It's okay," I told her. "You'll be meeting with the occupational therapist tomorrow morning right after we get you settled into your new home. I'll disconnect the stove so you don't set yourself on fire. Keep away from sharp objects in the meantime."

"Look," she replied. "I had to give a final exam at eight this morning, and…"

"And," I continued, "you stayed up last night reading your cat-detective book until I finally took it away from you and turned out the light. It was quite a struggle. You pouted."

"It's the end of the term. I'm in tough shape."

That I can readily agree with. As befits her family tradition she's worked like five slaves this term. Records fail to reveal that anyone in my family ever died of overwork, but Natalie's grandfathers emigrated from the fields of southern Italy to work in the steel mills of Pittsburgh, and fundamentally she's no different. She toils endlessly in the sulfur mines of Ohio University for her students and for the school, which depends upon her innate common sense and unassailable personal integrity to assist with decisions over curriculum and strategy that could tax Solomon.

Work continues at home. Students call in every half-hour to ask about projects and exam questions while she sits at her computer, calculator in hand and cat in lap, working through the equations. The first set of exams to be graded already lies stacked in her briefcase, and tomorrow she'll thrash through each solution from each student, trying to eke a bit of partial credit out of even the worst of their efforts. My job is to supply soda, coffee, and general encouragement.

"I could have made lots of money selling them the questions," I told her. "I read this article about corruption among faculty spouses. It's great."

She sighed. "I already told them what would be on the test. And I know you: if you knew what the questions were you'd tell them for free."

She's right. Anyway, the students don't need me: they're earnest seniors in a very selective program. These are kids who frequently dress up to go to class, and well they might: Wall Street financial firms hire them upon graduation, and even as some banks fail, others are paying Natalie's students signing bonuses.

Some belong to a stock-trading club she started. The members, all undergraduate students, work as semi-pro stock brokers, researching good stock buys and submitting their ideas to the club's student directors. Once Natalie signs off, the Ohio University Foundation buys or sells stocks according to the recommendations. Her kids consistently beat the market and major brokerages, turning $1 million into $1.5 million in three years.

It is the very definition of work: night after night the kids work in their computer-studded office, its overhead TV tuned to the financial channels, and Natalie looks after them. Meanwhile, I'm home digging in the garden or writing about refrigerators for a children's magazine. For all her academic celebrity Natalie has remained a firmly domestic creature—except when it all starts to fray at the end of each term.

And that's why I'm here. She's finally quit for the night, but presently a call comes from upstairs: "Could you come up here and stay with me until I can sleep?"

I'm on my way.

Making new friends through technology

"I can't fall asleep," called the small voice from upstairs. This was serious, for it was already long past her bedtime and Natalie had to rise early for her school's graduation ceremony. And so the Sleep Team assembled and lay there in her boudoir: me at her side issuing my usual complaints and comments about life, the young cat G Webster curled at her feet and the fluffy cat Amanda on her stomach, flipping a long feathery tail. Thus do we talk her to sleep each night. I know it's working when the patient's responses become fewer and less rational. It grew quiet.

And then the telephone rang. Natalie lunged for it, because by international treaty the telephone must always be on her side of the bed. The livestock hastily departed, landing in a hissing pile on the floor. "You have to push the button, but which button is it?" exclaimed my short spouse more articulately than her condition should have warranted. She flourished the telephone around, trying to peer at it closely in the dark, and finally reached for the switch on the bedside lamp.

Our new cordless telephones seemed like a great idea until tonight. The original one was for the dining room, where telephone cords were always a problem. Then we found another cordless phone—they're inexpensive and reliable now—for our office, where the Mardi Gras beads that hang from the floor lamp can tangle with printer's data cable, and one less cord is a blessing.

And we bought one for Natalie's room to foil G. Webster, who at one point in his kitten development was fascinated beyond all restraint by curly telephone cords. Neither hiding it in books nor stringing it upon the bedside lamp could prevent him from wrestling the cord and the telephone attached to it into submission onto the floor and thence under the bed.

But our particular cordless telephones require that you push a button marked Talk when you answer it or you'll be speaking into an unresponsive block of Malaysian electronics. And the location of that button on this phone was different from the one in the office, and also from the one in the dining room, and Natalie was technically asleep.

"Okay, gimme it." I gruffed. "You have to push the big button in the middle."

"Well, it's different on the one downstairs," she replied.

I pushed the button. "Hi," I spoke into the device.

"This is Christy the nursing supervisor," replied the cheerful voice at 12:25 a.m.

"That's good," I said. "We're feeling fine. What can we do for you?"

"What part of the hospital are you in?" she asked.

I looked around for a moment just to make sure. "Well, right now we're lying in bed on East Mulberry Street. At least I thought we were."

Further inquiries determined that nobody we knew was sick and that Christy and I were victims of an errant switchboard somewhere that rang both our telephones and then left us to figure it out. This can happen when a bit of high-frequency interference overwhelms the system's error-correcting circuitry. We wished each other a puzzled good night and turned back to our separate worlds.

Other star-crossed couples, they say, have fallen in love and married after an operator plugged into the wrong circuits. But tonight I wished only for my late mother-in-law's thick Italian accent: "How you?" she would have inquired with her unfailing courtesy, and nothing was better for terminating an errant connection.

"How you?" I said to Natalie, and we broke down in laughter.

"I think I can sleep now," she said.

CPSIA information can be obtained
at www.ICGtesting.com
Printed in the USA
LVHW092155051119
636490LV00001B/130/P

9 781494 781361